Lines of Power

Limits of Language

Gunnar Olsson

University of Minnesota Press
Minneapolis • Oxford

Published by the University of Minnesota Press
2037 University Avenue Southeast, Minneapolis, MN 55414
Printed in the United States of America on acid-free paper

Library of Congress Cataloging-in-Publication Data

Olsson, Gunnar, 1935-
Lines of power / limits of language / Gunnar Olsson.
p.   cm.
Includes index.
ISBN 0-8166-1949-2
1. Languages—Philosophy.
P106.O845   1991
401—dc20   90-24070
                                                            CIP

A CIP catalog record for this book is available from the British Library.

The University of Minnesota is an equal-opportunity educator and employer.

Wassily Kandinsky, *Intimate Communication* (Oval No. 1), 1925. Oil on canvas, 36 × 31 cm. Photograph courtesy Musée National d'Art Moderne, Centre Georges Pompidou, Paris.

Horizontal-vertical structure with contrasting diagonal and point tensions—scheme for picture *Intimate Communication* (1925). Wassily Kandinsky, *Point and Line to Plane*, Diagram 24.

CATALOGUE

RESENTATION

S

INDEX

•

PRESENTATION

Indivisibly thin

Nowhere

Time and space. Common knowledge and intimate feeling. Now-here, no-where. Hyphen at work. Striptease in hiding.

Such is the story of the pages to follow. A head on a platter, a collection of essays from the decade of nineteeneightyfour. Remembrance of creativity and socialization, erasure of categorical bounds, throw of dice into the social space of silence, eye setting mind to rest, lines intersecting at points of insight. What is the difference and how can I know about the same? A question mark as a point under an S in a mirror. An I as an I no matter whether reflected or turned upside down. Solipsism as the ultimate honesty. Impossible to say, easy to show. The taboo of the taken-for-granted, the myth of the norm.

The show itself is an exhibition of invisible lines, wrinkles of laughter covering traces of sadness. In the intimate communication there is a family resemblance, faint recognitions of Johan Asplund, Franco Farinelli, Ole Michael Jensen, Johannes Møllgaard, Allan Pred, José Ramirez, Dagmar Reichert. With friends like these, living is a pleasure.

Dematerialized

We live forward and understand backward. This explains why in retrospect I can detect exciting parallels between the development of my own work and that of Wassily Kandinsky. As he once had reacted to Monet's *Haystack,* so I now wonder if it would not be possible to get further in this direction.

● ● ●

W.K.   *The geometric point is an invisible thing. It is the most ultimate and the most singular union of silence and speech. It belongs to language and signifies silence. Only its concentric tension discloses its inner kinship with the circle—while its further characteristics rather point to the square.*

GO   Outwardly the point is physical expression. Inwardly it is the
          tension of maximal/minimal meaning.

W.K.   *Theoretically, a work of art can, in its final analysis, consist of a*
            point. The simplest and briefest is that of the centrally placed point—of the
        point lying in the center of a surface which is square in shape:

This therefore represents the prototype of pictorial expression.

GO   The point is the proto-element of the graphic, hence of thought
          itself. To understand is to condense a thought-position into a point and
        place it in relation to other points.

•

W.K.   *The geometric line is an invisible thing. It is the track made by the*
            moving point. The line is, therefore, the greatest antithesis to the pictorial
        proto-element—the point. When a force coming from without moves the point in
        any direction, the line has the tendency to run in a straight course to infinity. The
        simplest form of the straight line is the horizontal. In the human imagination, this
        corresponds to the line or the plane upon which the human being stands or
        moves.

GO   Outwardly the line is physical expression. Inwardly it is the
          relations between its constituting points. *Along* the line, points touch
        points and thereby produce a tension of silence/speech. *In* the line, its outer
        edges touch nothing and therefore produce a tension of meaningful/
        meaningless.

W.K.   *Horizontal lines are black, vertical are white. Just as horizontals and*
            verticals are silent lines, so black and white are silent colors. A sufficient
        example of this is our black mourning and the white mourning of the Chinese.

Dematerialized

This perhaps sheds an especially strong light upon the difference between the inner nature of Chinese and Europeans. After thousands of years of Christianity, we Christians experience death as a final silence, or, according to my characterization, as a "bottomless pit," whereas the heathen Chinese look upon silence as a first step to the new language, or, in my way of putting it, as "birth." The horizontal-vertical cross consists of one warm and one cold line—it is nothing other than the central position of the horizontal and vertical. Of course, every phenomenon of the external and the inner world can be given a linear expression—a kind of translation.

GO   In the origo of cause-and-effect lies the silence of the taken-for-granted. In the horizontal lines of the equal sign is the consistency of reasoning, of one point leading to another.

W.K.   *The diagonal is the most concise form of the potentiality of endless cold-warm movement.*

GO   To begin speaking, the horizontals and verticals must be tilted. The most talkative line is the diagonal. This is Samuel Beckett's Unnamable.

W.K.   *Even the straight line, in the final analysis, carries within it the desire to give birth to a plane; to transform itself into a more compact, more self-contained thing. The spreading out, especially in the case of a short, straight line, bears a relation to the growing point. Here too, the question "When does the line as such die out, and at what moment is a plane born?" remains without a definite answer. The boundaries are indefinite and mobile. Everything here depends upon proportions, as was the case with the point—the absolute is reduced by the relative to an indistinct, subdued sound. In practice, this "approaching-of-the-boundary" is much more precisely expressed than in pure theory. The "approaching-of-the-boundary" is a potent source of expression, a powerful means to ends in composition. Both edges of the line are to be considered as independent outer lines.*

GO   Approaching-the-boundary is the only way to learn. This can be

Dematerialized

done from the outside or from the inside. Outside is body, inside is mind. Touching is an individual speech, feeling a social silence. Approaching-the-boundary is taboo, for it is in the boundary that the tree of knowledge has its roots.

●

W.K.   *The term "Basic Plane" is understood to mean the material plane which is called upon to receive the content of the work of art. The most objective form of the typical BP is the square—both pairs of boundary lines possess an equally strong sound.*

On approaching the boundary of the BP, a form increases in tension until, at the moment of contact with the boundary, the tension suddenly ceases. The point of intersection of the two diagonals determines the center of the BP.

GO   In the corners of the square lie the points of intersecting horizontal and vertical lines. These are extreme concentrations of the tension of speech and silence. At the center of the Malevich square is the point of indifference.

●   ●   ●

It is to the dematerialized point of abstractness that this volume aspires.

POINTS

Sermon of Remembrance

This recoiling recollection of self-portraits is a tribute to the god Janus. Janus is a pivoting symbol of gate-keeping, whose major characteristic is not that he can see in opposite directions at the same time, but that he is able to merge seemingly contradictory categories into a meaningful whole. In the same evaluating glance of the present he can catch a glimpse both of those pasts that once were and of those futures that have yet to come.

Janus's concern is with creativity. This makes him a deity of our own time, for the crucial presumption of modernity is that creative praxis grows out of criticism: while created objects appear fixed, they are in deed temporary; while creative activity seems always in flux, it is in fact permanent. Thing yields to process, stability to change, certainty to ambiguity, noun to verb, being to becoming. And yet, even Janus himself is hung on the momentarily stable reality of the present. The time is therefore now, for in actuality there can be no other time. In the tale I am about to tell, the present is nevertheless doubly tied to the memories of the late 1960s and to the prospects of the twenty-first century. Poised in the middle is the symbol of 1984.

In the Sisyphean mood of modernity, I shall strive to place myself inside Janus's head, well remembering from Nietzsche that it was not God who created man in his image, but Man who created god in his. From that privileged position I shall try to experience how Janus makes sense out of the logical contradictions he sees around him. What I would really like to understand is how he manages to deal with double bind in such a fashion that he is celebrated as a god and not put away as a schizophrenic. My examples will seem to come from that special case of thought-and-action that is Swedish state capitalism. In reality, though, I shall illustrate some principles of forgetting, for even though parts of what I write reflect what I know without knowing, the most crucial fragments are those I have forgotten without remembering that I forgot them.

If my distortions happen to be further distorted in the reader's mind, then so much the better. The reason is that I will then have helped creativity along, for creativity never stems from the perfect rerendering of simple truths but always from the errors inherent in every translation. It is at those moments that interpretation can yield to interpenetration and subjective ambiguity be allowed to rule over objective certainty. Translation without a "me" is therefore impossible. It follows that the meaning of my words reign over yours and that is regardless of whether the sign "me" denotes the writer or the reader. The central purpose of this volume is consequently to show some aspects of the collective unconscious as this revealed itself during the second half of the twentieth century. Ideology critique is another word for the same activity. My tribute to Janus is not in glorifying him but in being so immersed in his spirit that I cannot do with it.

CONFESSION
OF SINS

Science is an integral part of modern mythology. Like other myths it aims for truth, defines truth, and supports truth. Obeying its ritual I must therefore specify a set of preliminary definitions.

To define is necessary, for without shared definitions our thoughts-and-actions are anchored in the ever-shifting nothingness of solipsism. And yet, to define is to take the first step toward the fallacy of misplaced concreteness and the alienation it embodies. Thus, to define is to distinguish what is inside a boundary from what is outside it; it is to split open a natural whole; it is to sift friend from foe like wheat from chaff; it is to employ an intellectual technique for grasping and communicating what is otherwise nongraspable and noncommunicable; it is to use Ockham's razor on Samson's head. But in prison, Samson's hair grew long again, and in the revenge of the end he killed more Philistines than ever before.

According to the *OED,* to define is "to bring to an end," "to state exactly what (a thing) is," and "to declare the signification (of a word)." All definitions involve elements of thingification and are therefore well ingrained in the current metaphysics of presence. But the necessary Cartesian separations are never more than the first step in the recognition of the

Sermon of Remembrance

interdependence of subject and object, self and other. For bridges to connect, there must first be a rift: Whatisculturehidinginthesilentspacesbetweenitswords?

But to define is not merely an intellectual necessity. It is also an issue of making others accept my cleaving categories. Whenever I do, I exert power. As a consequence, I shall hope to write-and-act in such a way that I erase my original definitions. Yet, whatever is erased always leaves a trace. And so it is that this first chapter of my intimate journal is loosely patterned after the liturgy of the Protestant church. Thus, I am already in the midst of a collective confession of sins (admitting the impossibility of staying within given categories). I shall then proceed to a confession of faith (defining what the specific congregation takes to be its categorical boundaries). After that I will move on to the reading and explication of the Gospel text (applying the definitional principles to the special case of my own development). Finally, I end with renewed prayer that our trespasses be forgiven.

Oh, to sin is to trespass. To trespass is to cross a boundary. To cross a boundary is to break a definition. To break a definition is to create. To create is to be different. To be different is to sin. To sin is to live in self-reference.

So, Janus! Help me become a sinner! Let me understand how you break definitions! Teach me how to erase what others see as irresolvable paradoxes! Teach me the equation of that third lens inside your head whereby you transform contradictory images into coherent wholes!

Speak, memory, speak!

As memory speaks, it should nevertheless be remembered that my memory is like that of everybody else. What is crucial is not what I remember but what I forget. Memory has little to do with what once was, more with what is right now, most with what is left for the futures that never will be. In this perspective, memory appears as a hypothesis yet to be rejected. Memory's claim on universal acceptance has less to do with what now happens to be true and more to do with techniques of legitimation. As if to prove my point, the Greek word *alētheia* meant "true," whereas its opposite, *lēthē,* meant "forgotten." Etymology itself suggests that remembering is a sanctioned technique for purifying our individual and collective conscience. By telling half-truths now, I make it easier to tell whole-lies later. And yet, a new time has just begun, for what else can time ever do. Heads chasing tails, tails chasing heads.

CONFESSION
OF FAITH

In the disciplinary environment of postwar Sweden, there were tight ties between geography and planning. If not then, then at least now, I believe that this coalition between science and politics is a modern strategy for wielding power, not only over space but also over time, not only over oneself but also over others. I believe planning to be a political and bureaucratic phallus symbol, whereby the present penetrates the future. I believe that to plan is to preserve what now is by transforming fleeting intentions into unyielding stones of physical and institutional structures. Values of the strong today are ontologically metamorphosed into the facts for the weak of tomorrow. The result is a modern version of the castration complex in which some fear the loss of something they once had, while others experience the lack of something they never possessed. Thus, from the

Sermon of Remembrance

suppressor's elevated perspective, planning appears as a thoughtful way of extending a heritage of hopes and fears from one generation to another. From a different perspective, it shows itself as an efficient technique for raping the future. From either perspective, it is like other cases of penis envy: inseparable from authority.

The authoritarian elements of planning play over hierarchical organization levels. The main issue concerns the welfare functions of different decision units and how these are traded off against each other. As a consequence, planning interferes deeply in the dialectic between society and individual, a fact that posits planning in the holey cross between the social sciences and politics; none of these activities poses a more central question than that concerning the relation between individual and collective, one and many, subject and object, I and you, us and them. Myth shares the same concern.

It will be evident in later chapters how my conception of geography-and-planning leads to issues of power, as does my understanding of ideology. But what exactly is that untouchable for which people kill and get killed? What is the structure of those belief systems that require some architects to build Auschwitz and others to construct dehumanized apartment complexes and commuter trains? What are those forces that reflect and influence the ontological transformations through which things turn to relations, relations to things?

These questions are in the spirit of Janus, for they are questions of ideology critique. They are therefore themselves part of that ideology of modernity that artists like Marcel Duchamp have lived and expressed. And yet, they are all embedded in the classical definition that takes ideology to be a form of social philosophy that aspires to merge description and prescription, theory and norm. An ideology is therefore a system of coherent beliefs, whereby we try not only to understand the world as it is but also to change it into what it ought to be. It follows that different ideologies express different sets of internal relations. Ideologies bring theory and practice together and enable us to distinguish permissible from nonpermissible, go(o)d from (d)evil, Heaven from Hell. It is in the nature of all ideologies to be thoroughly dialectical: they forge together what logic says is contradictory and they include what conventional categories exclude.

CHOIR

My definitions of ideology and planning are closely related. Both activities are nourished by the legitimating interplay of mystification and domination. It follows that planning is an ingredient of that ethical glue whereby the is of the past and the ought of the future are bound together. Everyone has his ideology, for without it he would not know how to dis-member the world into graspable pieces and then re-member it into a whole again. Crackpots crack pots, potters pot cracks.

There are few writers more ideological than Karl Marx; not only did he understand the world, but he changed it as well. His fundamental insight was that the two verbs "is" and "ought" are dialectically consumed in the ideology of the ruling class. Already in the first sentence of *The German Ideology* he and Friedrich Engels symptomatically wrote that "men have constantly made up for themselves false conceptions about themselves, about what they are and about what they ought to be." It is consequently in the collective unconscious that human action is harmonized with the possible, just as the possible arises in the interest of the status quo. But, as Ludwig Wittgenstein later came to note, this harmonizing legitimation is neither intentional nor conscious, for intentions are thoroughly embedded in their situation, in human customs and social institutions; intentions are in internal relations and thereby in the belief systems that support and reflect them. Saying that an actor has evil motives is therefore deeply misleading. The situation is rather like that of classical tragedy, where everything is right in the beginning and everything wrong in the end. But nothing is on purpose, because in reality beginnings never reach their end even though ends always grow out of beginnings.

To understand human action is never to blame. It is instead to recognize that every actor is so entrenched in his role that he takes the shadow play to be reality and reality to be the play. It is indeed an integral part of all internal relations (and thereby of all ideologies and all mythologies) that we obey their commands without hearing them, and without knowing where they come from. To break the spell completely is impossible, for under the mask I shed there is always another. And the next veil I always fail to notice because it is one with my own sight; I see the mote in my neighbor's eye, but not the beam in my own. Perhaps the fashion of today's ideology critique is nothing but a legitimating activity for modernity itself.

The internal relations of mystification and domination were never as skillfully disentangled as in Marx's critique of fetishism. Since he conceived of money as the fetishist commodity par excellence, he saw the money form of things as a reflection and determinant of what he called "the categories of bourgeois economy." With his dialectical mind he could grasp how the seemingly contradictory forms of use and exchange value exposed nothing but different sides of the same commodity. The major shortcoming of the men who hitherto had made up false conceptions for and of themselves was that only one of their Janus-eyes had functioned; their thing-eye could see, their relation-eye was blind. And so it comes that the captives of current ideology are better equipped to explain the things and use-values of a commodity than to understand relations and exchange values. But in the more insightful mind of Janus, the relations connecting the labor of one individual with that of the rest appear not as direct social relations between individuals at work but as what they really are, material relations between persons and social relations between things. It is a characteristic of those in power that they have internalized this ontological law of the double so well that they automatically turn it to their advantage— unconsciously, unwittingly, and often unwillingly.

But even though I have recognized some of Janus's features in Marx, the history of Marxism is different. Instead of conceiving action as a game of ontological transformations, practicing Marxists have preferred to fit social and economic reality into the categories of dialectical materialism. But in the real world of qualitative leaps, two times two can sometimes become five, just as in some geometries parallel lines can sometimes cross. And so it is that Hegel and Riemann, Marx and Einstein, all have something important in common. What they share is a concern with severed relations and a pursuit of categories gone astray; while Hegel and Riemann formulated new principles of thought, Marx and Einstein used these alternative reasoning modes for catching and ordering new sets of material data. Their collective spirit loomed high in my own generation of young geographers in their sixties—unconsciously, unwittingly, and often unwillingly.

GOSPEL   Although beginnings never reach their end, they nevertheless indicate the degree of belief I have in the future: "in the beginning was" is the beginning of myth; "once upon a time" is the beginning of fairy tales; "in the end" is the beginning of the being of nothingness.

For the truth of the decade, now turn to the Gospel text. It comes from the *Book of Lines,* chapter 1132, verses 1980-90.

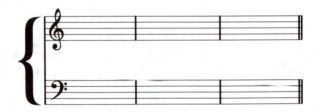

TEXT   Eggs in Bird   Certainty/ambiguity
       Joyce

                            Prison

       Hegel   Creativity/socialization
       Kant

                            Trust

       Russell   Name/description
       Sophocles

                            Tragedy

Beckett Mallarmé	/	Individual/society
	Silence	
Barthes Lacan	—	Signifier/signified
	Body	
Girard Kandinsky	☐	Point/line
	Power	

PREACHING

Janus's message is in the white spaces of the text itself. They connect stages on life's way and in this sense they silently speak for, of, and to themselves. Perhaps they should be left alone. But without the white spaces there would be no black marks to notice. And with no intersecting lines there would be no portraits to exhibit, no story to recite.

In the beginning was the double volume *Birds in Egg/Eggs in Bird*. It was published in the city of London in the year of 1980 and it contained a report on my adventures of the previous decade. The human condition was here conceived as a constant struggle between the forces of certainty and ambiguity. Gradually there emerged the experience of living in a prison-house of language built with walls of the taken-for-granted. Even though this prison is escape-proof, one can nevertheless bend the bars and catch a glimpse of the other side, tempting and mad at the same time. There is a desire beyond naming, a fooling around, a Joycean vicus of recirculation.

The current volume contains notes from the prison, explications of the Gospel text. In retrospect, I can now understand them as strange illustrations of Wassily Kandinsky's theories summarized in his *Point and Line to Plane;* departing from the Kantian origo of stability and change, creativity and socialization, my thoughts eventually curl up in a form resembling that of a Malevich square. In essence my studies are experiments performed on straight lines, themselves serving as objective correlates of abstract relations.

The first lines are the " = " of the equal sign. In my own story, they begin in questions of trust and end up in a theory of human action structured as a tragedy. The issue concerns the relations between proper names and definite descriptions and my major companions were Sophocles and Bertrand Russell.

The second line is the "/ " of the unnamable in-between, another word for the void between individual and society, you and me. There is in this line a social space of silence shared by Stéphane Mallarmé and Samuel Beckett. In my own mind, it is the two essays of this section that remain the most intimate, rich and dear.

The third line is the "—" of the Saussurean bar. As I let the thickness of this mark between signifier and signified approach zero and infinity, I move from words to body, asking you with my eyes to ask again. Once more the issue is one of trust, conviction, taboo, and predictability. With Jacques Lacan I am not yet at ease. With Roland Barthes good memories remain.

Viewed together, the lines themselves get cornered into points of power. From the turning and twisting of these correlates emerges a set of figures hitherto unseen. Perhaps they are mad. But perhaps the penumbrae, the squares and the cones, together contain seeds of a valid theory of human action. Too early to start. Too late to end. Time and space may well catch the physical. For the rest they do nothing.

COMMUNION   And so it came about, that which never may happen. There is a sense of an already-but-not-yet built into the decade of which this book itself forms a part. Its relations to Swedish ideology are obvious and spelled out in the companion volume entitled *Antipasti*. More hidden, and hence more important, is the international community of spirited geographers. Through his sensitive ear, Franco Farinelli teaches me more than I know. And Babble's walls come mumbling down.

BLESSING

> Conventions die more slowly than
> revolutions. As revolutions fade away,
> recollections fill the caveats. Rebels, however,
> have a passion for Russian roulette. Some win,
> some lose. It is significant that Diana was
> Janus's favorite; when peace came and she
> could return to the temple, he closed its gates.
> In self-reference, silence speaks through the
> culture which fills its empty spaces. Praxis is
> totalization, totalization is praxis.
>
> For nothing spake to me but the Fair face
> of Heaven and Earth, when yet I could not
> speak: I did my Bliss, when I did silence,
> breach.
> SPREACH, Janus, SPREACH!
>
> And there was an erotization of Euclid.

Popilius the fornicator

The castration and the mirror

The sea and the times
always begin anew

The penetration of Popilius

Figures after Pol Bury, *Le sexe des anges et celui des géomètres,* pp. 91-93.

Creativity and Socialization

With this second introduction, I want to illustrate the workings of the dialectical principle of self-conscious reevaluation. The inevitable anchoring is in the here and now, even though that nowhere is doubly tied both to my own experiences from the past and to my hopes and fears for the future; by necessity every author is an inventive individualist.

As usual, I shall say nothing new, merely reformulate some of the old.

• • •

With this purpose, I now proceed to yet another set of preliminary definitions. What is creative research? What is research training?

Most commentators define research as the production of new knowledge. To be called scientific, this new knowledge must be steeped in

n that makes it cumulative. And already with this requirement follows a
Jamental contradiction: How can I say anything new in a language of
accumulation? How can I tell the truth about a world of constant change, if I
am forced to use words with stable meanings? What happens when the
deviant is normalized?

This problem of language and knowledge is at the core of all research
training. What is graduate education, if it is not an introduction into a mode
of communication characterized by very particular rules of pragmatics,
syntax, and semantics? In this perspective, research training shows itself to
be what it really is: a gigantic language course, an element in the
reproduction of the currently dominant ideology.

It follows that whereas research sometimes can be creative, research
training is always conservative. It is for this reason that most dissertations
tend to say less about the world than what the world through its
dissertations says about itself. In conclusion: There is a contradiction
between creativity and socialization. Just as the overriding aim of the
former is the creation of the new, so the overriding aim of the latter is the
preservation of the old.

In this perspective, knowledge becomes an issue of translation. The
strategy is to restate a point in another form, even though it is well known
that perfect translation is impossible. And by an ironic twist we often
discover the new not through the perfect translation we aim for but through
mistranslations acutely reinterpreted. It cannot be repeated too often: Every
translation says less about the subject matter it refers to and more about
the culture in which it is expressed. Not even in the language of science is
there a one-to-one correspondence between word and object. Modern
theories instead argue that words refer to other words, not to concrete
things. Signs embrace. Signs copulate. It is from the union of signs that
novel meanings bubble up, for meaning is not a material but a social
phenomenon. It follows that a text can be neither read nor written outside
its own context. The concept of self-reference becomes a key to
understanding, the liar's paradox a paradigmatic case.

Within this framework of postmodernism, text and context are in
constant intercourse. The dilemma is that the words that link them together

are never new words. Instead they are old words, inherited from old texts and old contexts; our expressions are not innocent virgins but highly experienced whores, as ready to use as to be used. And so it is that understanding a text requires a kind of psychoanalysis, not of the personal relations of the reader/writer but of the cultural relations of the words themselves. Expressions are put on the couch. Etymology becomes a tool in the archaeology of meaning.

But even though atomistic words are important, the relations between them are even more crucial. The cumulative ability of the scientific language is therefore less in the semantic stability of reference and more in the syntactic properties of the logical constants. The secret of an equation is not in the imaginative interpretations of its x, y, or z, but rather in the close reading of its pluses, parentheses, and equal signs. As a rule, these constants follow the principles of conventional two-valued logic. And yet the very point of dialectics and many-valued logics is to demonstrate that there exist alternative formalizations that are not based on the law of the excluded middle. The question is whether these alternative reasoning modes have the capability of producing cumulative knowledge.

This question in turn leads to an issue that has been a source of continuous puzzlement. It is simply put: Why is it that we know so much more of physics, engineering, and medicine than the old Greeks, while of politics and love we may know even less? Why have we accumulated knowledge in some disciplines and not in others? Recalling that all learning comes through translation, how do I interpret this difference? Is the deep structure of mathematics more isomorphic to the deep structure of the physical sciences than to that of human affairs? Perhaps!

Another indication is that the classical opposite of truth is not falsity but forgetting. Is the true merely the re-membered? What do we search for in our re-search? Is research itself a religious ritual paying honor to the mythology of origin and making sacrifices to the metaphysics of presence? Why are we putting more emphasis on our premises and conclusions than on the reasoning rules themselves? Why are we more interested in results than in processes, more in sticking to stable categories than in transcending them? To which extent is this demand a consequence of the

Creativity and Socialization

goal of knowledge accumulation? How do I grasp the dialectic of creativity and socialization? How do I teach my students to be obedient and disobedient at the same time, to be true to given categories yet to transcend them? Is understanding inconceivable outside the realm of categorization?

YES!

With this YES, the dilemma stands naked before us: to categorize is to fetter. Not to categorize is to leave the world in incomprehensible chaos. Reformulation: to categorize is to draw a boundary; to create is to cross a conceptual limit. Conclusion: to create is to sin. And yet: to tell the truth can sometimes be an evil, to lie can sometimes be a duty.

●

Emerging from these inquisitive remarks is the idea that in *Birds in Egg/Eggs in Bird* became my main message: The *human condition* is a relentless struggle between the forces of *stability and change,* universal and particular, outer and inner, certainty and ambiguity, truth and forgetting. Even though research tends to legitimize itself as an objective search for knowledge about visible phenomena, it is in fact a subjective search for ourselves. As a consequence, the contradiction surfaces anew, for it is clearly written into our research manual that the investigator should remove himself, that he should see only what others can see as well. But as an individual I am unique. Why then am I taught to be dumber than I am?

At the heart of this attitude lies the problem of recognizing something when I see it again; the art is to sense the stability in the change. This in turn is the *logical* problem of *identity* and *difference.* On the most fundamental level, the question is how I can make a statement which at the same time is both true and informative; $a = a$ is obviously true but as a tautology noninformative; on the contrary, $a = b$ is informative yet obviously false. Bertrand Russell was grappling with this issue throughout his life, and his resolution is in the theory of proper names and definitive descriptions. According to that theory, an identity statement is both true and informative if the equal sign is flanked by a proper name on the one side and a definite description on the other:

$$Venus \; = \; the \; morning \; star$$

and

$$Venus \; = \; the \; evening \; star$$

In addition, the statement is both true and informative if the equal sign is flanked by two definite descriptions of the same physical object:

$$the \; morning \; star \; = \; the \; evening \; star.$$

What mattered most to Russell was to uphold the spirit of the *Leibnizian* salva veritatae; a true statement about an object is not to be affected by the name I assign it. The crux of the matter is, however, that whenever I preserve truth through reformulation, then I am inevitably back in the thorny issues of translation. In particular I must face the fact that what is a definite description for me might not be a definite description for you. Whose description should I strive to preserve? Who is more important? I or you? We or they? The presented or the represented?

Creativity and Socialization

Via these powerful questions it becomes clear that the inquiry which started as a characterization of the human condition and then moved into the logic of identity now has reached the level of ontology. Thus, whereas the issue of logic is that of identity (how do I recognize something when I see it again), the issue of *ontology* is that of existence (how do I know whether what is in my mind is in yours as well). The classical distinction runs between what Frege called *reference* and *sense,* Meinong termed *existence* and *subsistence,* and Quine labeled *transparent* and *oblique contexts.* Oversimplified, the distinction is that when I talk about a physical object both you and I can point to it and thereby agree that we are talking about the same thing. But when I refer to my intentions, hopes, fears, and other beliefs, then this type of sensual sharing is more difficult. Thus I cannot be certain that my belief statements are identical to yours. The issue of ontology consequently involves physical things on the one hand and mental relations on the other. In essence, it is an issue of communication; even though ontology is concerned with what is, it is in reality about the relations between one and many.

So it is that the issues of the human condition, of the logic of identity, of the ontology of existence, all come together on the level of *mythology.* For in mythology there is no question more central than that of the many and the one, of *society* and *individual.* What now is research training? Yet another element in those intricate socialization processes through which individual and society become mutually adjusted.

I have already argued that the mythological language of science contains a strong bias such that the concepts of stability, identity, reference, and society are favored over their dialectical counterparts of change, difference, sense, and individual. The tender discourse between order and adventure is being stifled by the very language in which knowledge is accumulated. How do I break out of this descriptive/truth-functional/thingified idiom that is the hallmark of conventional science?

●

From these preliminary beginnings spring questions of epistemology.

How do I learn? How do I teach? Which text could serve as a mythological springboard? What should follow if not the beginning?

Therefore: Bend your heads and read the following fragments from the script anew:

> In the beginning God created the heavens and the earth. The earth was without form and void, and darkness was upon the face of the deep; and the Spirit of God was moving over the face of the waters.
>
> And God said, "Let there be light"; and there was light. And God saw that the light was good; and God separated the light from the darkness. God called the light Day, and the darkness he called Night. And there was evening and there was morning, one day.
>
> And God saw everything that he had made, and behold, it was very good. And there was evening and there was morning, a sixth day.
>
> Thus the heavens and the earth were finished, and all the host of them. And on the seventh day God finished his work which he had done, and he rested on the seventh day from all his work which he had done.
>
> But a mist went up from the earth and watered the whole face of the ground—then the Lord God formed a man of dust from the ground, and breathed into his nostrils the breath of life; and man became a living being.
>
> And the man and the wife were both naked, and were not ashamed.
>
> Now the serpent was more subtle than any other wild creature that the Lord God had made. He said to the woman, "Did God say, 'You shall not eat of any tree of the garden?' " And the woman said to the serpent, "We may eat of the fruit of the trees of the garden; but God said, 'You shall not eat of the fruit of the tree which is in the midst of the garden, neither shall you touch it, lest you die.' " But the serpent said to the woman, "You will not die. For God knows that when you eat of it your eyes will be opened, and you will be like God, knowing good and evil."

Such are the words written on the first pages of the Book that is its own culture. To me they provide the most concise summary of the principles of creativity and socialization; what becomes so clear is that epistemology turns into *ethics,* that modes of learning involve issues of *good* and *evil.*

But what did God do when he created? Exactly what we do today! He—because the creator is almost always a thundering symbol of masculinity—followed a simple two-stage procedure. First he used his flashing sword to cut the chaotic void in two. In his solitude he then sorted the severed parts into different heaps. Beginning in chaos he ended up in order; through his categories he brought cosmic form onto chaotic void. This first step is a lonely endeavor. To categorize differently is an instance of individual action.

In contrast, the second stage of creation is in the social anchoring of the new categories; the order that resulted from the adventurous cut is legalized; individual practice becomes collective praxis. What God did was consequently to codify the split by giving his categories official names. With his muscles he did nothing, merely leaned back into his easy throne, puffing on his Freudian cigar. "Let there be!" And there was! Light and darkness, air and water, fish and fowl, man and woman. In pairs of two, all flowed with the smoke rings out of his mouth. The Creator did not build the world, he uttered it. Likewise the Genesis is not about God but about Man, not about mystical spirits from other times and other places but about you and me, here and now.

It is for this reason that questions of research and research training provide such good illustrations of the relations between individual and society. More explicitly, the activity of categorizing is essentially individual, the naming essentially social. And yet, this powerful connection between individual and society is itself taboo. If not, then why did God forbid his children to eat from the tree of knowledge? What would it look like, a world in which everyone could play the role of God separating good from evil? Without shared symbols there could be no understanding, without understanding no agreement. Without agreement there could never be accumulation.

And so it is that all socialization processes deal with the epistemological issue of normalizing the deviant, or rather with the taboo of the limit between the two categories. Since creativity lies in the non-normal of statistical deviation and the socialized in the mean of the normal, it is not surprising that the ideology of welfare capitalism has led into a gigantic crisis of creativity. For it is a governing thought not only of scientific reasoning but also of welfare capitalism that the deviant must be normalized. And yet. Already Emile Durkheim knew that the normal cannot survive without the deviant and that the individual who breaks a moral code is sanctioned. Indeed I have gradually come to believe that the well of creativity swells up from the dialectical contradiction between the normal and the deviant. The creative individual eats his own social shit. Perhaps it is in this perspective of creativity that both the anal complex and the castration complex become most interesting; the relations between the theses of Protestantism and Luther's visits to the privy are well analyzed.

●

Inherent in everything I have written thus far is the idea that creativity and socialization reflect and are reflected by the dialectical and internal relations between individual and society, deviant and normal, variance and mean. Yet it should be noted explicitly that these relations are fundamentally antireductionist. Internally and dialectically related statements are indeed so intricately interwoven that everything hangs together with everything else; the truth of "$3 \times 3 = 9$" is an integral part of the truth of "$3 \times 7 = 21$" and of "$7 \times 7 = 49$."

Nobody has written better on these issues than G. W. F. Hegel. At the same time his discussions are often incredibly obscure and open to several interpretations. Thus it is difficult to state in a positive manner what dialectics is. It is easier to state what it is not.

Dialectics is not a method whose aim is to arrive at predictions. Neither is it a method for arriving at firm, forever valid categorizations. It is rather a sort of systematized insight into the process of learning, especially into the revelation of the hidden in a surface feature. Dialectics is not an explanatory logic, even though explanatory logic forms its necessary starting point. In essence it is an understanding epistemology. As a consequence, dialectics does not look ahead into the future, only back into the past. It is not a language of commands through which fluctuating becoming is forced into stable being, but a mode of life through which hidden mechanisms of freedom, suppression, and submission are lured into the open.

In this perspective, it is not surprising that dialectics sometimes has been called the algebra of revolution. Such a characterization is nevertheless misleading, a fact that vulgar Marxists always misunderstood; even though the two activities of understanding and making are closely related, they are never the same. Personally, I believe it is more difficult to understand the world than to change it. Nowhere was Marx more wrong than in his eleventh Feuerbach thesis.

●

The discussion thus far is a play with the following elements:

Human condition	*stability/change*
Logic	*identity/difference*
Ontology	*reference/sense*
Mythology	*society/individual*
Ethics	*good/evil*
Epistemology	*normal/deviant*

Already this brief recapitulation illustrates how Hegel's epistemology is driven forward by the two concepts of construction by negation and self-conscious reevaluation. The former is of course close to Jacques Derrida's concept of deconstruction and there is no coincidence that some of Derrida's most creative writings come from a penetration of the emptiness between Hegel and Nietzsche. Understanding leads to liberation but also to the recognition that even when earlier thought positions have been erased, they always leave a trace. In the process, identity and difference show themselves as two sides of the same coin.

The best illustration is in Hegel's well-known discussion of master/slave. Suffice it to say that both the master and the slave arrive at a stage of *aufgehoben* understanding when each of them realizes that the one cannot do without the other. And so it is that the process of self-conscious reevaluation never stops but forever continues. A stage of final synthesis is therefore completely alien to genuine dialectics. There is no realized utopia, for dialectics is itself part and parcel of the self-centered search of modernism.

In my mind, dialectics grows out of the border area between individual and society. The reasoning somehow rests within itself. As a consequence, subsequent thinkers have tried to extend and concretize the Hegelian heritage. Karl Marx and Søren Kierkegaard are good cases in point, for both tried to find a firm foundation on which to put Hegel's thoughts to rest.

Marx sought and found his anchoring point in society. He arrived there via his analysis of material things and via his value theory. His starting point was in the concept of the commodity. It was this notion that he squeezed so hard that it gradually changed and then suddenly revealed itself as something qualitatively different; the spade he was digging with changed into a use value. But when the same spade was squeezed even harder, it showed itself to have an exchange value as well. Upon analysis, the spade consequently turned out to be not only a material thing but also a social phenomenon; material and social relations come together when the individual digger learns that he cannot exist outside the society of which he is a part.

Kierkegaard chose another route. Thus he found his anchoring point not in the general which surrounded him, but in the specific of himself. Writing under pseudonyms he managed to purify his positions. Toward the end of his life he could even transcend the opposing arguments and approach an *aufgehoben* state: the choice between alternative views and life forms is a choice that no one can make in your stead. The choice itself involves a leap into the inherently unknown. We learn by moving backward; we live by moving forward.

● ● ●

I have argued that the relation between creativity and socialization is genuinely dialectical. The major contradiction runs between the normal and the deviant, the master and the slave, the powerful baptizer and the obedient congregation. Throughout, I have attempted to illustrate an epistemology of striptease and perversity, of deconstruction and deviance.

The discussion will now move on from the points of this distanced rereading of the seventies into the intimate lines of the eighties.

MAY THE GODS BE AGAINST US, FOR THOSE WHOM THE GODS ARE FOR ARE CASTRATED ALREADY FROM THE OUTSET.

LINES

On Doughnutting

Dealing with modal logic is like eating a doughnut from the inside. It is to chew away at fluffy possibility and to digest it into precise and agreed-upon knowledge. In the process, the black hole of Wittgenstein's *Tractatus* is gradually pushed to its outer limits, for on the logician's way toward silence, there is "nothing but the familiar idea of information as elimination of uncertainty." As the explorer learns to speak exactly about states of affairs that are other than the actual, then the known becomes credible, the believed plausible.

The question is this: Can the modal logician be trusted?

● ● ●

In the paper under discussion, Professor Hintikka merges his own formulation of possible-worlds semantics with a novel approach from game theory. His problem is that the number and complexity of possible worlds is too large to be grasped and comprehended; the wff's or theorems produced by the syntactic machinery leave the interpreter with too much to believe. Any sane person would go crazy for less.

It was as a prophylactic against this type of madness that Hintikka originally developed his model system and the semantics that come with it. The idea was to have the theorems doubly anchored, not only *within* the formal system but *without* it as well. Not even this double medicine proved strong enough, though. There remains an embarras de richesses, for the ideas of one man are not necessarily those of another. It is in this situation that Hintikka now suggests that game-theoretical semantics be applied as a brake on runaway possibility. The players of his two-person zero-sum game are named "Myself" and "Nature." The strategy is to win atomic sentences, well noting that the players are dealt not one card at a time but actually whole worlds of sentences. "Myself" wins G(A) if A is true, otherwise "Nature" wins. The point of the game is to discover the inconsistency of a sentence S, i.e., to elucidate the structure of logical (deductive) reasoning itself.

Despite assertions to the contrary, I doubt whether game theory will reduce significantly the impossible number of possible worlds. Anyone who tries to evaluate them runs the risk of going mad. It is this potential schizophrenic that the professor now prescribes therapeutic treatment for in Monte Carlo and Las Vegas.

My peculiar questions are not meant to divert interest away from the technical aspects of Hintikka's work. Indeed the opposite. For it is only by examining the minute details of the taken-for-granted that we can hope to unravel the governing techniques of social cohesion. And since logical reasoning is the most formalized form of social practice, it will perhaps yield its secrets more easily than other types of discourse. In this regard, the concept of deduction is similar to the concept of money. Indeed I cannot imagine a possible world that does not contain the notion of promising as one of its integral ingredients.

•

My first problem concerns the desire for *consistency* and thereby the moving force of deductive reasoning. The accepted approach is of course to produce a chain of arguments in which the truths of the premises are preserved in the conclusions. One proposition is perfectly translated into another as everything that follows is parasitic on whatever went before. Understanding is consequently a matter of expressing the new in the language of the old, for to know is to specify a translation function. If an error creeps into this reformulation process, then it shows up as a false conclusion.

On this rendering, logical discourse becomes a species of moral discourse. Deduction proves itself to be an act of obedience, a submission under sets of institutionalized rules. The conclusions turn out to be predictable not because they are inherently true, but because they reflect the taken-for-granted of social practice. Intention has little to do with it, for it is well established that obeying a rule is to follow it blindly. There can never be surprises. And thus it is that truth and society come together in self-referential yet evolving forms of life.

The immensity of possible worlds seems to be a function more of syntax and pragmatics than of semantics. At the same time, the habit of hooking formal reasoning to its premises appears as an insidious instance of a metaphysics of origin, a resort to the security of being and a flight from the fears of becoming. Logical deduction shows off as a kind of mythical narrative, proceeding from an axiomatic beginning to an inevitable end. It is not that the fantastics of counterfactuals and possible worlds are too much to believe, but that getting rid of them leaves too little to hang on to. No longer slowed down by the grapnel of causality, both individual and society would begin to drift like Flying Dutchmen on the open seas of imagination.

Even though truth-preservation is the stated goal of causal inference, practical inference is quite different. This is partly because the possibility of creating illusions, of cheating and deceiving, is an integral part of language itself. And herein hides both the threat and the driving force to truth. A lie can be reasonable, the reasonable can be a lie.

Plato knew it long ago. Hence his hatred of the theater. Derrida insists on it now: Truth is a woman, an umbrella on a dissection table. Temptation. Seduction. Who does what to whom, why, when, and where? Jaakko Hintikka's performative readings of Descartes come to mind as well, for there are "thought acts" just as there are "speech acts." Are sayings like "cogito, ergo sum" and "to be or not to be" inferences or performances?

In my mind they are both. The reason is that every utterance contains a crucial blending of self-reference and persuasion. There is in deed no description without performance, no thought without action. Even in the minimal semantics of a Donald Davidson or a Jacques Derrida, there remains a trace of speech act theory. Incredible truths are not truths at all, for truth is less an issue of what is the case and more of what is credible. Any narration is therefore a kind of thought experiment, an irresistible desire to produce a possible world. The trouble is that to be trustworthy is to be predictable. The deed and the doer are inseparable.

Click in the lock. Imprisoned again behind the bendable walls of language I become uncertain about the distinctions between language as the universal medium on the one hand and language as calculus on the other. But high in the sky I glimpse a kite, seemingly free like a bird, yet in reality tied down with invisible strings of social convention. Once more, the human condition reveals itself as a struggle between certainty and ambiguity, necessity and possibility. Modal logic is entangled in it all; possible worlds are everywhere, not the least in the Sartrean concept of Nothingness. In turn, this raises the issue of whether it is possible to have an author who is authentic and legitimate at the same time. Should Professor Hintikka's exploration be read as a collective opinion issued by the High Court of modal logicians or as an individual's piece of postmodernist fiction? But even if a lion could talk, I could never understand him.

In tragedy as well as in logic, everything is right in the beginning. In the end there may be a difference. Both art forms are nevertheless social acts permeated by a dialectics of good intentions and obedient behavior. In reasoning there are axioms and logical constants, human artifacts solidified in social practice. In tragedy, it is all fate. How can I act otherwise? Is it dishonest to break the consistency of one's own rules? Is the modal logician a tragic hero? Is Sophocles the father of a valid theory of human action?

"What therefore is truth?" asked Nietzsche in his essay "On Truth and Lie," and replied: "A flexible army of metaphors, metonymies, anthropomorphisms, in short, a sum of human relations, which have been poetically and rhetorically intensified, transformed, bejewelled, and which after long usage seem to a people to be fixed, canonical, and binding."

"Too much," sounds the voice of possible-worlds semantics. "I shall show Myself to have the power of winning over Nature!"

•

The game-theoretic approach raises issues about the *techniques* that Myself uses to convince Nature to change its mind and thereby lose its bet. Dangerous indeed. Since "Nature" is not Nature but a pseudonym of "Society," everything is up for grabs. Not only the atomic sentence of s_1, but the whole world of w_1. Not only existential things, but individualized forms of life. Not only wife and children, but God himself. Consistency is the name of that game in which even consciousness must find a common language. But "con-" and "com-" are variants of the same prefix meaning "together," i.e., "social."

In this common context of conning, who is the croupier of game theory? How can he be trusted? Why play at all, if to be trusted is to be predictable? Un coup de dés, Mallarmé! Champagne on the house! What is the strategy for winning: to be predictable or to be different? Is it more rewarding to mix genres than to stick to given categories? Is the optimal technique the Foucaldian one of reaching the heart of the matter by stretching the skin of its limits?

Perhaps. For the act of convincing is never direct but always indirect. There is a connection yet radical difference between reality and the words in which it is caught and recreated. Although experience may sometimes be immediate, understanding is always one step removed, a presentation of a representation. Alienation.

Could it have been this that Bertrand Russell had in mind when he insisted that "every proposition and every belief must have an object other than itself"? Who knows what he believed? Perhaps the reply is that every word is in a sense forward-looking, waiting for the answer it prompts. For even in Tallahassee, Florida, Philosophy's Hall of Mirrors is now turned into a narcissistic echo chamber, where all that is solid melts into air. As Max Black once put it: "Perhaps every science must start with metaphor and end with algebra; and perhaps without metaphor there would never have been any algebra." Not surprisingly, W. V. Quine turns out to be an expert on metaphoric persuasion. Yet it was not a modal logician, but Stephen Dedalus, who "prove[d] by algebra that Hamlet's grandson is Shakespeare's grandfather and that he himself is the ghost of his own father."

It is a function of metaphor to carry meaning from one level to another; to serve as a stereoscope of ideas; to create possible worlds; to be cognitive and creative at the same time. Theories are in fact metaphors of metaphors, all part and parcel of their own contexts. Indeed you choose your theory as little as your mate. Every discourse lives on its own boundaries where one word rubs its skin against another. My body is itself a metaphor.

In its own being, Bataille's *Story of the Eye* illustrates how possible worlds spring from a mating of precise words and ambiguous contexts. It seems significant that the Spanish term "huevo" in its ovary carries the double meaning of "egg" and "ball." Language that touches is neither blind nor insensitive, for as words copulate, possible worlds are brought into being. The plot of the mind is moved by the desire of the body. Nothing immaculate. Everything a self-referential play of ontological transformations. Words have their histories too.

And thus it comes that the eye and the index finger become metaphors for grasping the distantness inherent in all subject formation. My only contact with the world is through the holes of my body. It is through them that Myself is penetrated by the social norms of Nature. And vice versa. It is through them that you and I are made so obedient and so predictable. My body is my mode of existence. Therein lies the power of Myself. Therein lies the double key to certainty-and-ambiguity, understanding-and-persuasion, thought-and-action.

•

Now I follow Lacan and put the signifier on top of the signified. This is yet another way of emphasizing that to be creative is not to have an idea that searches for its expression, but to have an expression that searches for its meaning. Built into this attitude is nevertheless a risk of thingification, of giving too much to *existential quantifiers* and too little to human relations. Nouns are made to win over verbs. The game is not fair.

To illustrate, recall Hintikka's example:

(10.1) It is known to whom everybody bears the relation S, instantiated as (10.2) It is known whom everybody admires.

In the formal translations, the focus is on the words "whom" and "everybody." What is highlighted is *what* is being related. Left in darkness is the relation itself. This practice of reification is deeply rooted, because relations are ontologically alien to the ruling ideology of presence. Relations are invisible, silences inaudible. In society's interest of communication, there is a strong tendency to ignore fleeting relations by turning them to solid matter. How else could our words mean the same? By taking subjects and objects for granted, we automatically do the same with predicates.

Relations are not only relations between things but also between cultural words; not only words but concepts; not only concepts but meanings; not only meanings but other relations. Relations are always related to other relations, all twined into braids of strangely looping spirals. Self-reference is the term for this notion coiled at the center of current thought. The snake bites its own tail as modernism receives its postal prescript.

In the meantime, it seems more important *that* I admire, than *whom* I admire. Is my lover a fetish, my fetish a love? Is reification deification, deification reification?

•　　•　　•

Modal logic is incredibly rich. Too much? Or too little? Jaakko Hintikka's repeated fireworks are as ingenious as they are illuminating.

Hiding in the tivoli crowd, I have nibbled away at my doughnut. Smears in the face; crumbs in the moustache; licks on the lips. First, I wondered about consistency, obedience, and predictability. Then, I asked how the world simultaneously is grasped and altered. In the end, I ended in self-reference.

The riddle is why the doughnut did not give me indigestion. In search of an answer, I first went to Harry's Bar, where I sipped a Montgomery of remembrance. I then moved on to the Gritti Palace. And in the breeze from the opened windows, belief returned to the knowledge it had never left. The Contessa is the proof, for she knew at nineteen what the Colonel found out at fifty-one. Half a century of hard labor, across the river and into the trees.

The lesson seems clear:

To write is to walk on a pavement of citations. To read is to hear a hand whisper under a table. To explore possible worlds is to be a geographer with a mind that matters and a matter that minds. To gamble is to realize that every thought gives off a throw of dice.

Magician's Wand

And there was a long silence.

An awkward two pages came to pass between the chapter heading and the
first marks.

It is this brimming emptiness that at the same time kept you and me separated and united that I would now like to enter. I ask for your company in this void of the taken-for-granted, because it is here that we find some of the most crucial issues of the human and the social sciences. It is here, for instance, that we discover both the necessity and the possibility of prediction. But what is prediction if it is not a narrative—the telling of a story—leading from one expression to another? What is the theory of prediction, if not the practice of obedience? But nobody is perfectly obedient and hence nothing is perfectly predictable; there is a dialectic between law and order on the one hand and adventure and chaos on the other.

It is the workings of this dialectic that I tried to illustrate by the blank pages, seemingly lost and increasingly unpredictable. Was I ever going to print that essay that you had the moral right to expect? What a scandal it would be, if I had fooled you into buying a wordless book. No doubt, the University of Minnesota Press would have difficulties justifying its expenses of social money and personal kindness. Cause for litigation—the Press versus Professor Olsson. Future invitations withdrawn, for he who has not done the expected in the past cannot be trusted in the future; once a liar, always a liar. Such is the common verdict. And such is a major component of that ethical glue that simultaneously keeps individual and society together and apart.

It is the decomposition of this invisible glue that I see as the major task of a critical social science.

●　　●　　●

What I would now like to detect is the structure of that particular algebra that filled the emptiness of the nonwrinkled sheets. Although I do not believe that this algebra of silence has much to do with deductive reasoning per se, one may nevertheless learn a great deal by using it as a metaphor. The reason is that logical reasoning is one of the most formalized and hence exaggerated forms of social practice. By looking at that special case, we may perhaps gain insights into the forces of social cohesion in general.

The moving force of deductive reasoning is in the desire of consistency. The accepted approach is to produce a chain of arguments which is so constructed that the truths of the premises are preserved in the conclusions. Truth-preservation is the name of the game. One proposition is perfectly translated into another such that whatever follows is parasitic on whatever went before. The logician and causal reasoner is thus trained not only to anticipate the future but to control it; there is no surprise, merely blind obedience. Understanding is by definition a matter of expressing the new in the language of the old. If an error creeps into this reformulation process, then it shows up as a false—i.e., unreliable—conclusion. But to the logician and the conventional social scientist, a false conclusion is like a degenerate criminal, something to be detained, treated, and corrected.

What intrigues me is how the innocent baby of a true premise sometimes revolts against the rules of proper conduct and turns itself into a crazy yet meaningful conclusion. Which are the connections between your expectations when you first opened this book and the particular black spots which now meet your eyes, turn into words, and then stir around in your mental stew of taken-for-granted? I am intrigued by the conflict between the moralism inherent in the taken-for-granted of the reader's mind on the one hand and the unexpected event of this peculiar text on the other.

Who are the wardens in the prison hospital of mad conclusions? How do I recognize its inmates?

On this rendering, rule-governed discourse becomes a species of moral discourse. Deduction—whether formal as in the thought laboratory or informal as in this essay—shows itself as an act of obedience, a submission under sets of institutionalized rules. The question of truth is an issue less of science and more of jurisprudence. For what I have just exemplified are some trivial operationalizations of the concept of promise, hence of trust, hence of predictability. "Come, my child. Dare to jump! And I promise to catch you."

The lesson is that logical and scientific reasoning is a kind of mythical narrative that proceeds from an axiomatic beginning to an inevitable end. What we seem to practice is a metaphysics of origin in which the arrow of implication becomes a symbol of mimetic desire; two points expanding into a line. The gods of social cohesion demand their sacrifices. Now as much as then. Here as much as there.

•   •   •

There are offerings carried to the altar of mimetic desire. One victim of this practice is our critical understanding of human action itself. For even though the principle of truth-preservation is integral to the abstract theory of causal reasoning, it appears to be completely alien to the concrete practice of human action. For what is the point of creative action, if it is not to falsify what is now the case and to make true what is now false? Put differently, the essence of action is not to be truth-preserving but to be truth-creating. Action is less an issue of remembering and more an issue of forgetting. Action is by its very nature a matter of truth-transformation, a production of seemingly mad conclusions.

This situation actualizes a tremendous challenge, for the concept of human action is absolutely central to the common concern of human and social scientists. Human action indeed fills the same role for us as the nucleus does for the physicist and the gene does for the biologist. But I am equally convinced that any major breakthrough in the human and social sciences will go hand in hand with new developments in the syntax and semantics of a suitable sign language. No longer will any of the conventional truth theories do, for we must never forget our Nietzsche: Truths are illusions of which we have forgotten that this is so.

To tell a truth that is informative and not merely tautological is to act creatively. It follows that to tell the truth is to lie a little. Telling truths is not enough. Being convincing is equally necessary. But to be convincing is to be trusted, even when you are saying something that was never said before. "Why did you jump, my child?"—"Because you told me to, my father."

The secret I am trying to reveal is that truth is not an immaculate conception, but the fruit of an unholy union of logic and rhetoric, of holding fast and of letting loose. Like everybody else, I would like not only to grasp truth but to be believed when I speak it. The trouble is that to be trustworthy is to be predictable. The deed and the doer show themselves to be inseparable.

And that is why this essay began with some blank spaces of mourning. What I mourned was the loss of innocence. God's grace.

• • •

Via the concept of trust, the two fields of epistemology and ethics come in contact, not only with one another but with ontology as well. In particular, the concept of trust brings us into the twilight zone between the Cartesian categories of visible and invisible, things and relations.

Indeed I have come to categorize not only trust, but the broader notion of human action itself, as a game of ontological transformations. Human action is a bag of magician's tricks in which abstract content transcends itself into concrete form and vice versa. For instance, it is well known how untouchable ideology is turned into the bricks and mortar of architecture, which in its turn shapes our modes of thought, which then make us build in certain ways, and so on and on and on. Theoretical and political categories are likewise operationalized into statistical groups and legal paragraphs. As William Blake put it: "Prisons are built with stones of Law; Brothels with bricks of Religion."

But the visible and touchable thing of a stone has an ontological status that is drastically different from the invisible and untouchable relations of a law. Since we all can catch a stone with our own body, it would be peculiar to argue about its identity and existence. With the obligations of a law it is quite different. Why else would we have courts for settling disputes?

In conflicts between relational thoughts and tangible things, it would indeed be mad not to privilege the latter over the former. The consequent drift toward thingification is clearly grounded in the interface between communication and ontology. To communicate is to thingify. To thingify is to communicate. And yet, there is a fallacy of the common noun, for the world is not merely things, but something called meaning as well. And thus it is that the very stuff of understanding becomes its own stumbling block.

Perhaps it is even such that writing itself is the sign of the superfluous. How come being abstract enough is so unbelievably difficult?

I think the cul-de-sac answer to this forbidding question is that we live in a culture that puts more trust in statements about things than in statements about relations. If so, it becomes even more important to focus on the concept of trust itself, for without a proper understanding of this concept it will be impossible to decompose the glue that makes us hang together. Put differently: Which are the connections between ontological thingification and social obedience? Why did you feel so awkward at the beginning of this essay? Was the reason that you had nothing to tie yourself down with?

Is the explanation for your discomfort in the fact that physical expressions lack social meaning outside their cultural context? Did I as a writer behave in bad taste? For it is in fact only as elements in a complicated communication process that sounds become words, movements become gestures, clothes become signals. And thus it is that meaning is extracted not from tautological identities but instead from systematic differences. Once again, truthful meaning is impossible without a sprinkling of lies.

It is in this mythical dance of opposites that presence and absence, Being and Nothingness, begin to move with one another. How do I catch not the dancers but the choreography of that dance? How do I make you believe what you already know? Who is courageous enough to build monuments not in solid marble but in airy space—monuments as eternal as human action itself?

•   •   •

Having arrived at these questions of bodily means and cultural meaning, I now move into a brief account of how I came upon them. To do so, I shall add yet another footnote on human geography, for it is the frontiers of that artful science which this essay is meant to expose.

It should be noted immediately that *the* issue of geography has been to unravel the relations between form and process, between the geometric properties of resources on the one hand and human life on the other. The traditional approach has been to translate empirical observations into the spatial language of a map. In the next stage of the analysis, it is this map that is interpreted. Put crudely: From a description of spatial form one makes inferences about the processes of human life and action.

Through some sophisticated mathematical work at the end of the 1960s, we now know that this type of inference is not valid; the same spatial distribution can in fact be generated in drastically different ways. These conclusions led to devastating results, for they hit the disciplinary ship of geography below the waterline. Most of the crew nevertheless remains on board, unaware not only of the ongoing reconstructions but indeed of the damaging torpedoes themselves. This essay should itself be read as part of the reconstruction work.

One insight that became clear around 1968 is that what we happen to say in our apparently objective studies probably tells less about the phenomena we are talking *about* and more about the languages we are talking *in*. As a consequence, we began to be more concerned with patterns of thought-and-action than with the geometry of spatially distributed things. The mistake of the past had revealed itself as a tendency to stop the dialectical process of human life in its tracks, to turn invisible relations into countable things, to hold our subject matter fast by turning it into consistent form and frozen content. In every so-called fact there is a rhetoric of the law and the taken-for-granted.

It was by such means that the inherent ambiguity of reality had been distorted into seeming certainty, the abstractness of thought into the misplaced concreteness of things; but it is the significance of the dialectical process that the truths of today become the errors of tomorrow. In a sense we came to realize that we were hitting our heads against the ceiling of language, that we were caught in a set of reasoning rules that killed both us and our subject matter. The meshes of the reasoning net are so strong, because they are twined by threads of consistency. The challenge is to acknowledge, to show, and to communicate that there are other, perhaps more attractive, conceptions of consistency.

It is in this context that I have noted how the traditional conception of consistency permeates not only the science of deductive logic but also the art of tragedy. Already Sophocles knew that tragedy concerns the relations between possible worlds and ontology, between *de dicto* and *de re*. But he also knew that the dice of this risky game are not fair, but that they are loaded in favor of the touchable, the visible, the spatial.

In logic, in scientific reasoning, in tragedy, and in human action in general, the crucial question is this: How can I act otherwise? Is it dishonest to break the consistency of one's own rules? Is it to Sophocles we must return to find the impetus to a valid theory of human action?

● ● ●

Perhaps. For the very point of theory is not to stare oneself blind on the forms of manifestation but instead to grasp the meaningful connections. It is as an aid in this task that I now for the first time draw attention to the Saussurean concept of the sign. I do so here because this concept explicitly unites the Cartesian categories I have alluded to before. As recalled, we usually write

$$\text{sign} = \frac{\text{signifier}}{\text{signified}}$$

Looking at this expression, it is one part of it that attracts my attention more than anything else. Significantly enough, it is too important to have a common name. What I am referring to is the limiting penumbra through which signifier and signified are kept together and apart. It is to this hidden Bar of Categorical Meetings that I go to search for fractions of taboo-ridden phenomena and taboo-ridden insights. It is exactly in the abyss of this power-filled void that visible becomes invisible, untouchable touchable. It is here that presence meets absence, absence meets presence. It is here that the I meets the Other, full of dreams and full of realities. It is here that Descartes can be witnessed staring into his own mirror.

In my attempts to get insights into the Saussurean Bar, I try to operate on it as if it were a mathematical function. Since the normal procedure for grasping a function is to let it move either to zero or to infinity, I try to experiment with the bar in the same manner. Either I let it become very thick, as I did at the beginning of this essay. Or I try to make it very thin as I now intend to illustrate. But where do I find a case where the penumbra is extra thin?

• • •

One example is in the icons of the Byzantine church, those mythical pictures of the nonpicturable, those images that are not images but holy form-and-content united in one-body-and-one-spirit. Another and perhaps even more interesting case lies in the language of moral codes, for a moral code is nothing until I obey it. It is in the moral code that symbol and behavior become one and the same.

This is clearly the case in the act of promising itself, for promising is the classical example of a speech act. Thus when I utter the words **I PROMISE,** then I perform a work immediately in my speech. I do not merely move my lips and vibrate my vocal chords, but I put myself in a new social relation. The Saussurean Bar is here as thin as it can ever become. Not only are word and object the same; so are object and meaning.

Nowhere is this merging of inner and outer more outspoken than in the wedding ceremony. With my promise to love a person, for better and for worse, I tie myself into a system of common norms. Society, through its witnesses, keeps me under its gaze as I put the round ring around her stiff finger. Automatically the participating bystanders extend what they see into expectations of proper conduct. But my partner is wiser, for she knows from experience that it is easier to lie with the words you share with others than with the body that is yours alone. Hence the act must be consummated. Put differently: To increase its trustworthiness, the promise is doubly anchored. It is of one mind in the public, of another in the private; of one body in the chapel, of another in the bedroom.

A different but equally important form of promising is built into the concept of money, i.e., into the very language of capitalism. As recalled, it was Marx himself who wrote that "the relations connecting the labor of one individual with that of the rest appear, not as direct social relations between individuals at work, but as what they really are, material relations between persons and social relations between things." On this rendering, it is easy to find the place where money hides its secret. It is in the penumbra between the nominator and denominator of the Saussurean sign.

Marx's quotation points to the abracadabra of money, that fantastic invention through which we can do what the multiplication table tells is impossible: multiply pears and apples. How is this trick performed? Who waves the magic wand?

As an amateur, slow-motion, illustration of the trick, please consider the pictured note issued through the trust of the Swedish Bank. To

understand its powerful function, one must realize that it presents itself under two guises, confusing and difficult for ordinary people to keep apart. One guise is that of the brute, material fact. The other is that of the social, untouchable fact.

As a brute fact, this pictured thing can be characterized as a bluish piece of paper covered with sets of strangely drawn lines. Its chemistry is complicated, for it must be difficult to print facsimile editions. If that were too easy, we would quickly begin to consider the thing not as a symbol of obligations but as what it really would be: a useless piece of paper. And who is dumb enough to trust a piece of paper?

As an institutional fact, on the other hand, the picture is not merely a piece of paper. It is an important symbol. And like all symbols, it lacks meaning outside its own context. As recalled from the tales of Robinson Crusoe, the lump of gold and the pieces of stone he found on his lonely island lacked all value. When he returned to civilization, however, these useless things suddenly gave him the power of changing the social reality of a poor widow and her starving children.

One decisive difference between brute and social facts is in the techniques of breaking them. Thus I can destroy the brute fact by moving my hands, by tearing it to pieces, by crumbling it up, by throwing it on the

fire. But when these movements are interpreted not as muscle contractions but as social gestures, it turns out that I have done nothing to money as a social phenomenon. Through my act of violence, I have in fact strengthened rather than weakened the social power that money wields over me; every time I handle money and other promissory notes, I bind myself to others in new ways. I put my reputation, and hence my future, on the line.

It should now be clear that the institution of money is nothing outside a complicated network of promises. Some of these promises may have their roots in material realities from the past, but in essence they are instruments for penetrating the absence of the future. Money is important not for what we *have* done to receive it, but for what we believe we *will* do in spending it. The interesting question is whether the promises of money can be believed. If not, then the banknotes cannot serve as promises for what to expect.

The answer is of course that the promises inherent in the language of money cannot be believed. This fact reveals itself not only in the daily fluctuations of the monetary markets but—more important—through the political acts of inflation and devaluation. Thus, what typically happens in the case of devaluation is that the president or the prime minister goes on television. Through this medium the ruler then declares that from now on the Swedish krona shall be worth 10 percent less than before. What he does through this speech act is not to tear asunder the brute fact of a bank note as I just did in my fake illustration. What he does instead is to tear away one tenth of the social fact of that same note. Ten öre to the flames. The symbolism is unbelievable: to placate the gods of social cohesion, 10 percent of past promises are carried to the altar. Ignited, they rise to the sky as white smoke. Old sins are not forgotten, merely purified. As the words leave the ruler's mouth, the dictionary of international capitalism is immediately rewritten.

It is in this context that inflation appears as the incredibly serious phenomenon it is: not primarily as a sign of economic crisis but instead as a crisis in the social institution of promising. And this is despite the fact that the whole idea behind institutions like national banks and the International Monetary Fund is exactly to guarantee the promises issued in the language of money.

Once again: In what are the promises anchored? The answer is that they are anchored in themselves. And thus it is that also money is an example of a dialectical self-referential language. It is perhaps in the fascinating trading of futures that this postmodernist use of money can be seen at its clearest; it is here that the language of capitalism works at high pitch, screaming as it frees itself from its chains to the existing.

Bringing it all together, it seems that the *Wall Street Journal* and the *Journal of Symbolic Logic* are serving the same dual function of evaluating the current value of past commitments. I cannot imagine a possible world that does not contain the notion of promising as one of its integral ingredients. Wealth is not possessed, for wealth is not a thing. Wealth is performed, for not only is it a relation but a type of speech act. Wealth in deed has little to do with the spatial distribution of visible things and much to do with the taken-for-granted of untouchable social relations.

And thus there *is* a foothold in this debate: in the void that exists and does not exist.

• • •

This essay should be read as an experiment with the taken-for-granted of the social space of silence. First I tried to make this space as large, then as small as possible.

Most of the discussion has been in the drunkenness of the Saussurean Bar, for it is here that people can be heard speaking with the double tongue of a snake. Their language is a peculiar dialectic anchored partly in a metaphysics of origin, partly in a metaphysics of presence. I have been neither here nor there, but always at the point of becoming myself. After all, it is in the Saussurean Bar that magicians and tightrope dancers meet and perform.

• • •

Silence, please! Or the dancing actors may fall into the reductionism of this side or of that side. Or even more tragically: they might slip into the rope itself, cutting their balls in the middle of the act. The mirror stage and the castration complex are closely connected.

Silence, please! For all I have retold is yet another version of religious mythology, i.e., of word becoming flesh and flesh becoming word. Calling it "ontological transformations" did not change much. Or did it? Anathema! Anathema! Anathema!

Silence, please! Blare of trumpets! And the walls come tumbling down.

this is a point

Set Your Mind at Rest

The **human condition** is a relentless struggle between the forces of individual and society, particular and universal, mental and physical, ambiguity and certainty.

The former obey the principles of practical inference, dialectics, and ongoingness. The latter follow the dicta of scientific reasoning, categorical mathematics, and status quo.

•

As the **struggle** evolves, the forces are brought together in the activity of self-conscious reevaluation.

Self-conscious reevaluation is itself a dialectical enterprise that leads to personal and social change. Nowhere has this been better illustrated than in Hegel's unfolding of the lordship-bondage relationship. Thus, as the master realizes his dependence on the slave and as the slave discovers that the master cannot do without him, so they both come to recognize that servitude is in the subordination of one self to another. "Just as lordship shows its essential nature to be the reverse of what it wants to be, so too, bondage will, when completed, pass into the opposite of what it immediately is." It is through the transcendence of contradictions that the world is moved, just as it is in the labor for his master that the bondsman comes to know that he has a mind of his own. To become conscious of life is therefore to reflect upon the nothingness of death. Whoever searches for knowledge tries to understand who he is.

•

Some will see my activity as an exercise in falsification of institutional facts. Others will call it construction by negation. A few will agree that wrestling with paradoxes is the only way to learn. But most will merely move their lips, parrot the words, and shrug their shoulders. They are the ones who shall never understand, for they will never ask before they know the answer.

• • •

The *languages* of causal and practical reasoning are radically different.
For this reason, it is dangerous to extend the language of descriptive social science into the realm of prescriptive social engineering. The point is that if we construct a society on the basis of current thought and practice, then we confine ourselves to a world that reflects the particular conception of man inherent in the language of causal explanation. We will thereby impose on praxis a sterile strictness that it neither has nor ought to have. The result is a society that mirrors the language in which we describe it.
In that brave new world there are no dreams to dream and nothing to be sorry for. Thinking is at a temporary halt, for in adopting the categories of manipulation we disown our dialectics. What we create is not a society

Set Your Mind at Rest

where autonomous man is free to grope for his own becoming, but a world of being, inhabited by atomized and thingified men. The thought of practical reasoning is overtaken by the action of causal prediction.

•

The root of the problem is in **categorization,** for all thought, action, and language reflect what we take to be identical.

In conventional reasoning, the principle of categorization is in Leibniz's laws of identity and substitutability. These are themselves embedded in the law of the excluded middle. Everything is identical to itself and nothing is identical to anything else. Nothing is itself and not itself at the same time. And yet, inherent in this stringent definition is nevertheless an element of dialectics, for it is only by learning what something is not that we know what it is. Built into the positive is its own negation.

The categorical realm is governed by the law of the excluded middle. Here reigns the certainty of authoritarianism. Its subjects are sterile objects and stultified thoughts. Banned as outcasts are those principals of the future who feed on fuzziness and indeterminacy and produce evolving relations and qualitative change. In this land of confinement, human action is mechanistic, noncreative, and status quo preserving. Like the citizens of the dictatorships, its constituents are prohibited from transcending their boundaries. In its chambers of council, ideology has been overthrown by methodology. In the process, methodology has become ideology itself.

In the creative realm, the principle of categorization is in Hegel's law of the identity of identity and nonidentity. This is itself grounded in the negation of the law of the excluded middle. Nothing is limited to itself. Everything transcends itself through its opposite into something new. And yet, inherent in this flexible attitude is an element of categorical thinking, for it is only through knowing what something is and is not that we learn what it is. "But it is here as in the case of the birth of a child; after a long period of nutrition in silence, the continuity of the gradual growth in size, of quantitative change, is suddenly cut short by the first breath drawn—there is a break in the process, a qualitative change—and the child is born. In like manner the spirit of the time, growing slowly and quietly ripe for the new form it is to assume, disintegrates one fragment after another of the structure of its previous world. . . . But this new world is perfectly realized just as little as the newborn child." Dialectics is the algebra of revolution just as evolution is the driving force of dialectics.

Dialectics governs in the world of creative change. This is the realm of ambiguity, where every law and every being is transformed through the principle of construction by negation. The inhabitants of this land are footloose wanderers, whose erratic compass sometimes takes them to beautiful vistas and sometimes to disaster. But wherever they go, they strive to replace the ambiguities of search with the certainties of definite action. And yet, the dialectical groping would grind to a halt were it not for the future they imagine by projecting the current world beyond itself. The essence is therefore in the act of turning identity into nonidentity. Even the attempt to escape it is itself an act. As a consequence, action is both suffering and delight, just as the freedom that nurtures it. Thus, the ideology of dialectics can never be hidden. Its clothes are like the emperor's costume.

•

The struggle between **ambiguity and certainty** gives meaning to life.

Ambiguity is in the thought of practical reasoning. Certainty is in the practice of causal prediction. Both are equally necessary, for overemphasis on the former produces anarchy and strict adherence to the latter leads to the prison of status quo. To look at the world from only one of the perspectives is therefore to see a false picture. One part will be overexposed. The other will be left in darkness.

To act is to interfere in the dialectical battle of certainty and ambiguity. It is in the Galilean tradition of objectification to join the war on certainty's side. Some of its casualties are buried in the Gulag Archipelago, murdered by the czar who never learned his dialectics. The Aristotelian tradition has fought to preserve subjectivity by siding with ambiguity. Its victims are in schizophrenic infirmaries, punished because they categorize differently.

As in all wars between ultimates, victories become defeats. Thus, it is by allying himself with objectivity that modern man has increased his sense of society and decreased the sense of himself. By employing analytic techniques that assume all ambiguity away, he produces distorted theory and inhibiting practice. In this manner, the analyst forces the fuzzy aspects of human action into the categorical exactness of his thought. In due course, this practice leads the centralized bureaucrat into acts of thingification.

But the dehumanizing practices are not meant to be vicious. Rather they are consequences of the actors' well-intended attempts to facilitate communication. The reason is that when I refer to myself as a thing, then I make *oratio recta* or *de re* statements, which are easy for others to grasp and imitate. When I refer to myself as a person, on the other hand, then I make *oratio obliqua* or *de dicto* statements, which are open to multiple interpretations. It is therefore in society's interest to force our talk into the precise net of categorical reasoning. The advantage is that everybody recognizes what we are trying to say. The disadvantage is that in catching certainty we mutilate ambiguity. In the process, society, which was meant for man, becomes an end in itself. But even then, the individual refuses to be regimentalized. Despite the power of objectivity, most people continue to learn more in the privacy of her bedroom than in the pretence of his office. Happiness is to climb a tree and to bid a child good night. Making a living is merely to stage another performance.

●

The war continues. Both sides are right for both represent ultimates. Thought and praxis leap at each other's throat because they are different and yet the same. Certainty and objectivity fight on one side, ambiguity and subjectivity on the other. At stake are the relations between man and men, men and society, freedom and necessity. The strategy of both sides is to attack the adversary not for what it is but for what it is not. This strategy is itself based on the recognition that to know an ultimate is to know its definition of identity. Society, certainty, and objectivity categorize in one way; individual, ambiguity, and subjectivity in another. The two sovereigns are equally absolute. In their own lands they tolerate no deviance. And yet, neither has its powers from God. In both realms, the rule is to rule by decree.

• • •

Thought and action are reflected in language and every language is defined by its **equal sign.**

In the drama of reasoning, the equal sign plays two roles. One is to denote identity, the other to denote existence. In both cases, the purpose is to tie the reasoning down to an ultimate. In this sense, the equal sign serves the same function as the anchors of a ship. It grounds our thoughts and actions and keeps them from drifting into obscurity.

Moving with the tide is anarchy, for what moves with the tide is not anchored to a definite ultimate. This makes the equal sign a purveyor of knowledge, for what it does is to anchor the ship of reasoning to a point whose bearings can be determined and agreed to. Nobody can do without the sign because it is the mechanism whereby we clarify to ourselves and others what we think, do, and say. It is the means by which we signify what we take to be the same. It is the basis of communication.

The anchors of reasoning can be constructed in many ways. Some are good for some purposes, others for others. Indeed we shall need them all, not to be used at the same time but rather to be deployed in intricate sequences. In one storm, a ship firmly tied to the unyielding will be torn apart. In another, a drifting ship will be thrown against the shore or be condemned to the high seas. In both cases, the fate is foredoomed. It is a choice between being wrecked or being a Flying Dutchman.

Conventional reasoning, dialectics, and modal logic all differ in their definitions of the equal sign. The former is in the pay of objectified society. Its virtue is in facilitating interpersonal communication of facts. The latter serve the subjective. Their advantage is in communicating insights of personal understanding. The former manipulates things. The latter manipulate thoughts.

•

The problem of **identity** is to recognize something as the same again.

In conventional reasoning, the equal sign is in the definition that a and b are identical if a and b have exactly the same properties. Identical words refer to identical things. The same labeling word must always refer to exactly the same phenomenon. What is called one thing is never called another. The advantage is that others will know what I hold as identical because they can see when I point to it. The disadvantage is that while categories are frozen, the world is not. Whatever we say will therefore convey more information about the language we are talking in than about the world we are talking about. And yet, the words we are talking in reflect the world we are talking about.

Conventional reasoning is the mode of short-term power because it is the language of status quo. It is incapable of catching the relations of qualitative change. This is a serious problem, for the man is not the boy and the acorn is not the oak. And yet I continue to respond to the name given to me at the ceremony on that Sunday morning I cannot remember. The anchor chains of categorical reasoning are consequently so strong that they tear the world asunder. This is despite the fact that Frege interpreted identity not as a logical constant but as a relational expression. The strength of Leibnizian identity is in what it is. Its weakness is in what it is not.

In dialectics, the equal sign is in the fleeting characteristics of functional relations and qualitative change. The meaning of a word changes with the phenomenon it denotes. A word has one meaning in one context and another in another. As a consequence, it is difficult to know whether what I consider identical is exactly what you consider identical. Every category includes both itself and its opposite. Statements in dialectics will therefore say more about the worlds we are talking about than about the language we are talking in. And yet, the worlds I am talking about reflect the words I am talking in.

Dialectics is the mode of long-term influence because it is the language of constant revolution. In this language, the nouns are batlike words that sometimes appear as birds and sometimes as mice. Yet they are neither, for whatever feature they take on is bestowed upon them through verbs like *aufheben,* transcend, and become. These verbs are performatives, which have the power of turning a slave into a master and a master into a slave. Although both faces are contained in the same noun, they emerge only through the activity of self-conscious reevaluation. Nouns are dead. Verbs are alive. Thingification is death. Action is freedom.

Double meaning is the strength of dialectics. It is also its weakness, for where the wind blows there goes the meaning. For this reason, there is little wonder that masters like Hegel and Marx have been criticized for their peculiar use of language. Misunderstandings abound. Most of them stem from the reader's unwarranted assumption that every writer must adhere to the Leibnizian definition of identity. But the dialectician has his own definition. As a consequence, it is not clear when a particular word is to be seen as a bird and when as a mouse.

Speakers of dialectics and conventional logic fail to understand each other. The main reason is that they anchor their words differently. Both languages are internally consistent. Yet they are both paradoxical. Thus the consistency of the conventional thinker makes him inconsistent, just as the inconsistency of the dialectician makes him consistent. The problem is consequently not with the thinking writer, who merely follows the laws of his land. It is rather with the preconditioned observer, who refuses to break out of his own mode of thinking, acting, and speaking. When he encounters a different way of structuring the world, he does not understand that familiar words are used in radically different manners. It follows that we can speak only to our fellow inmates. They are the only ones who share our categorical framework. This is the reason that even if a lion could talk, we could not understand him.

Both sides are wrong because both are right. There is indeed no one identity puzzle to solve. Instead the puzzle has two parts that refuse to come together. One part is made of flexible ambiguity, the other of staunch certainty. The materials are too different to be handled by the same tool. And yet it is in the interface between the two parts that the human struggle becomes exciting and worthwhile. Thus, it is exactly in this no-man's-land that we discover new thoughts to rethink, new dogmas to demythify, and new practices to alter. This is Russell's area of proper names and definite descriptions. Any words we use there are secured by two rather different identity anchors. The certainty side is fastened to the Leibnizian rock of meaning substitutability. The grapnel of the ambiguity side is sunk into the Husserlian quicksand of egocentricity.

●

The problem of **existence** is to recognize when what is in your mind is what is in my mind.

In conventional reasoning, the existence part of the equal sign is in the requirement that our statements be truth-functional. The labeling words must have direct counterparts in the world of physical phenomena. Thus, the conventionalist anchors his reasoning in the physical existence of the things he refers to. What counts is therefore what can be counted. What can be counted is what has a name. What has a name can be learned by everybody. What I count is consequently what you can count as well. And yet, nobody can see what he has not already conceived.

Conventional reasoning is the mode of thingification. It is incapable of catching the creative relations between thought and action. Thus it cannot acknowledge that what distinguishes the worst of architects from the best of bees is that the architect first raises his structure in his imagination before he erects it in wax. At the end of every labor process is therefore a result that already was in the mind of the laborer. It follows that whenever we speak about human creation, we speak not only about physical acts, but also about mental activity. Physical acts are in things. Mental activity is in hopes and fears. The former can be counted. The latter cannot.

The conventional existence requirement makes it impossible to deal with the mental aspects of creative change. In addition, it becomes difficult to speak both about the future, in which the things we talk about do not yet exist, and about the past, from which the traces of some events have already vanished. Hence the truth status of statements about the future is indeterminate, for even though the things I refer to may subsist in my mind, they do not exist in their body. The truth status of some statements about the past is likewise, for what I see from my particular vantage point in the present is only what illuminates that present. Tense is therefore important because in moving from the present to the future, parts of reality turn into nothingness and others into existence. We cannot judge a man's life until he is dead.

In dialectics and modal logic, being is not confined to the existing. Meaningful discourse is not limited to what is truth-functional and extensional. The rule is that some words are anchored in real objects that exist, while others are tied to ideal objects that subsist. It follows that existence remains in the things to be counted. Subsistence is in the mind. The problem is that you cannot name what is in my head. Therefore you cannot count it. There is no way to ensure that what is in my head is in yours as well. And yet, since nothing can come of nothing, neither you nor I can conceive what we have not already seen.

Dialectics and modal logic are languages of the mind. Validity is anchored in what I think. What I can measure, touch, or smell is for the conventionalist. Again, the motive force is in the verbs and not in the nouns. As a consequence, the dialectician and modal logician is more concerned with what I believe and do than with what can be seen in the objects themselves. It is important to realize that what is in the mind might forever stay there. But then it may not, for sometimes it is extended into action. It follows that subsistence is not condemned to eternal subsistence. It often transcends itself into existence.

To ignore the workings of the mind is to side with certainty. This is an understandable choice that is nevertheless mistaken. It reflects the desire to anchor our reasoning in unyielding rocks, open to public inspection. In the case of subsistence, on the other hand, I cannot guarantee that my words are in the public domain. But that does not mean that they are less significant, only that mental and physical objects lead different existential lives. The main distinction is that I can pat the poodle who lies on my parents' carpet, but I cannot pat the devil that sprang from the kernel of the Faustian poodle. But to say this is not to agree with the conventionalist who sometimes argues that talk about mythical things is talk about nothing. Nobody can talk about nothing. It follows that it is meaningful to say that it is false that my wife is bald, just as it is true that Cinderella had a beautiful shoe. Yet, even when I call my pussycat an ugly duckling, she continues to hunt chipmunks. But then, when I call my wife an ugly duckling, she does not do the same as when I call her a pussycat. This illustrates that things are dead while relations are alive. Things are in names. Relations are the essence of acts. Words can change people. To things they do nothing.

The speaker who anchors himself in existing things is understood by everybody. His anchorage is in the public domain. The situation is different for the speaker who ties himself to matters of subsistence. His statements of beliefs and relations are oblique. Hence the distinction is that the truth value of propositions about existing objects is in the objects themselves, while the validity of propositions about subsisting objects is in the mind of the speaker. Once again, the problem is not with the careful thinker. Instead it is with the reader who is so preconditioned in favor of the actual that he fails to recognize a new thought when he encounters it. The reason is that all thoughts are relations and that all relations subsist. But what subsists, many refuse to see because they cannot count it. The problem is in mixing modalities.

As in the identity case, both sides are right because both sides are internally consistent. And yet they are both wrong, for neither can communicate with the other. One speaks the tongue of ambiguity. The other writes the symbols of certainty. The two combatants have their words tied to different ontological stuff and their anchor chains are constructed from different identity principles. The side of certainty is fastened to the stuff of existence. Its chain is that of extensionality. The side of ambiguity is coupled to subsistence. Its chain is made of intensionality.

Language, thought, and action are rooted in ontology. Since ontology tells what belongs to the world, it determines what bases are available. Ambiguity makes one choice. Certainty makes another. Both sides are correct, for both are internally consistent. Yet both are wrong, because both are externally inconsistent. While the categories of certainty are so narrow that they always are falsified, the categories of ambiguity are so broad that they are always right. The battle will never have a victor, for even though the troops are constantly on the move, they never engage. There can never be reconciliation, for compromise leads to everybody's deprivation. The observer can therefore learn little by watching the troops from a distance. Instead, she must strive for the *aufgehoben* state of being audience and performer at the same time. When she does, she may well move beyond the optimism of Hegelian subjectivism and Marxian objectivism into the either/or dread of Kierkegaard. It is at that stage that we may finally realize that the drama of the human condition is a play of predicaments in which we are damned if we do and damned if we do not. When the activity of self-conscious reevaluation has reached that high point, then at last we are ready to learn. The reason is that the structure of predicaments is similar to the structures of paradox and tragedy. From that vantage point it becomes clear that man's knowledge is his ignorance. There is no affirmation free of doubt and there is no hero free of a traitor. We can come to terms with neither, if we do not come to terms with both. And yet, it is one thing to know the other language. Understanding how to live it is a different matter, for what is irredeemable is the measure of meaningless in meaning.

●　　●　　●

Any reasoning is anchored in its own ultimates and any duel between ultimates leads to **tragedy.**

●

The tragedy of Oedipus Tyrannus is in his **relentless pursuit of** knowledge no matter where it leads him.

In the beginning, Oedipus, who once saved the city from the Sphinx, is asked to become equal to himself again. This time he must save the city from the plague. Solving the riddle of the Sphinx led him to the dignity of man. Solving the problem of the plague shall take him to himself. In his search, he is pushed to truth by his blindness to truth. When he finally sees it, he blinds himself, thereby to see more clearly. At the end he saves the city but destroys himself. Neither result is on purpose, even though the search started with a purpose. It is all fate, except each step is itself avoidable. Necessity and freedom are mixed. Certainty and ambiguity come together. In the beginning everything is right. In the end it shall all be wrong.

●

Oedipus's problem is to understand the relations between **proper names and definite descriptions.**

His task is to establish an equation in which the identity statement is both true and informative. What is to go on one side of the equal sign is specified at the outset by Apollo, who in Oedipus's own account

> Sent us back word that this great pestilence
> Would lift, but only if we established clearly
> The identity of those who murdered Laios.

This specification seems clear enough even though it will later lead to horrible fears and futile hopes. Not many, but one, killed Laios. The mistake is not inevitable, however, because early in the play Teiresias, the blind seer, tells what must go on the other side of the sign. His words are clear and hardly ambiguous. He spits his message to Oedipus,

> I say that you are the murderer you seek.

And yet, the original specification is not so wrong. Like everybody else, Oedipus fits many descriptions.

Teiresias's prophecy is too serious to ignore and too damaging to believe. As a consequence, he is cursed, accused, and called a fool. He shouts back,

> A fool? Your parents thought me wise enough.

Upon this Oedipus halts himself. His anger turns into curiosity, his curiosity into fear. Like a bird shot in flight, he cries and wonders,

> *My parents again!—Wait: who were my parents?*

Before Teiresias leaves, he answers. He specifies in detail all the identities Oedipus will need in order to solve the problem and save the city. He even goes to the trouble of warning that what is now in Oedipus's mind is not in the facts. Thus he argues,

> *The man you have been looking for all this time,*
> *The damned man, the murderer of Laios,*
> *That man is in Thebes. To your mind he is a foreign-born.*
> *But it will soon be shown that he is a Theban,*
> *A revelation that will fail to please. A blind man,*
> *Who has his eyes now; a penniless man, who is rich now;*
> *And he will go tapping the strange earth with his staff.*
> *To the children with whom he lives now he will be*
> *Brother and father—the very same; to her*
> *Who bore him, son and husband—the very same*
> *Who came to his father's bed, wet with his father's blood.*

The very same. That is identity. Identity is the very same.

The chorus, not yet knowing whom to believe, offers no advice. The singers simply reflect,

Bewildered as a blown bird, my soul hovers and cannot find
Foothold in this debate, or any reason or rest of mind.

The mind of the chorus drifts. It is not tied down, for it does not know the identities. As it wanders, it sometimes sees a king and sometimes an incest-ridden murderer. The chorus is not to be faulted, for how could they know. Even in Oedipus's own mind nothing has yet become the very same.

In Teiresias's mind are the words of the Oracle. In Oedipus's mind are the memories of his attempts to make the Oracle's prophecies untrue. Thus, what is in one man's head is not in the head of the other. What Teiresias can see clearly is in Oedipus only obliquely. To remove the ambiguities, Creon, the potential successor to the throne and the man who hates anarchy, makes a plea for certainty. He advises that

You cannot judge unless you know the facts.

The same plea is later echoed by Jocasta. She begs Oedipus not to anchor his thoughts in his fears but rather in her facts. Hence first her advice

Set your mind at rest

and then her own version of what happened to her husband and child:

Now you remember the story: Laios was killed
By marauding strangers where three highways meet;
But this child had not been three days in this world
Before the King had pierced the baby's ankles
And left him to die on a lonely mountainside.

Creon's and Jocasta's point is that ambiguity is in the mind. But the mind must not be trusted. Security is instead in the certainty of facts.

The idea of Jocasta's proof is to show that the Oracle was wrong before. Hence it can be wrong again. Her proof was well intended, for it was meant to quiet Oedipus's forebodings. But this was not the effect. Instead, Jocasta raised an idea in Oedipus's mind. The idea was a fearful premonition, grounded in the past and projected into the future. He exclaims:

How strange a shadowy memory crossed my mind,
Just now while you were speaking; it chilled my heart.

What chills Oedipus's heart is the thought that his own previous curses may be turned against himself. This thought is that he himself may be the murderer, already sentenced by his own words. The source of fear is that Jocasta's account agrees too well with his own memory of how he killed the stranger at the crossroads. Indeed their stories differ in one detail only. The discrepancy is in the number of men who did the killing. The sole person who can settle the uncertainty is the single man who escaped. He must be called back immediately, for as Oedipus sees with frightening clarity,

> *If his account of the murderer tallies with yours,*
> *Then I am cleared.*

What is to be checked is therefore not Oedipus's mind, but Jocasta's facts, for

> *"marauders," you said,*
> *Killed the King, according to this man's story.*
> *If he maintains that still, if there were several,*
> *Clearly the guilt is not mine: I was alone.*
> *But if he says one man, singlehanded, did it,*
> *Then the evidence all points to me.*

Solving the equation now depends on a quantitative measure. The answer is in the determination of a constant. Once that has been settled, then the identities will have defined themselves.

What seems so straightforward is soon to be confused again. Hope is created by the messenger from Corinth, who brings news that King Polybos, the man who brought Oedipus up, has died. Jocasta is jubilant, for Polybos was not killed but called away by old age. She introduces the messenger to Oedipus with the words

> *He has come from Corinth to announce your father's death!*

To this the messenger replies,

I cannot say it more clearly: the King is dead.

In her blindness to the other face of the messenger's opaque statement, Jocasta raves. Once again she argues that what is in the mind does not count. Instead what is in the facts must be honored. She consequently repeats her plea to Oedipus that he must strike Teiresias out of his mind. Indeed, she goes even further, denouncing not only the soothsayer but the gods who sent him. She asks,

Why should anyone in this world be afraid,
Since Fate rules us and nothing can be foreseen?
A man should live only for the present day.

Have no more fear of sleeping with your mother:
How many men, in dreams, have lain with their mothers!
No reasonable man is troubled by such things.

In Jocasta's mind, reason is in things for things represent certainty. Ambiguity dwells in dreams and fears. They are for the man who does not know himself.

At this point, the vagueness of the oblique statements is about to be removed. With the irony of tragedy, truth is again revealed not for its own sake but with the purpose of relieving Oedipus of his dread. Thus, when he still refuses to go back to Corinth for the fear of sleeping with Polybos's wife, the messenger tells him that he has nothing to fear, for

Polybos was not your father.

With this the problem no longer is how to save the city from the plague. It is not even a question of who killed Laios. Now it is an issue of who Oedipus is. Under his relentless pursuit, the initial problem has changed. Oedipus's question is now a matter of life and death, guilt and punishment. What Jocasta had almost convinced Oedipus to be a true identity no longer is, at least not if the Corinthian messenger is correct. Since that would be too painful to acknowledge, Oedipus refuses to believe him. Instead he orders the messenger to substantiate his proof. This can be done by showing that in the equation Polybos is nothing but a zero, which can be ignored in all calculations. This is done expeditiously when the messenger says that Polybos was

No more your father than the man speaking to you.

But not even this is proof enough for the shaken Oedipus, who exclaims,

But you are nothing to me!

to which he finally gets the reply,

Neither was he.

Zero is equal to zero is equal to zero. Even after the double check, nothing is equal to nothing. But in Oedipus's logic, nothing is nothing. To say that his father is nothing is therefore absurd. Nobody, not even a king, can have nothing as a father.

After the Corinthian's revelations, the statement that links the proper name "Oedipus" with the definite description "the son of Polybos" is no longer a true identity. Instead it is suggested that the true and informative identity is in Oedipus's own name. This becomes clear when he asks the messenger, who turns out to be the very same that once gave the baby to Polybos,

From what did you save me?

to which he receives the reply,

Your ankles should tell you that

and subsequently the elaboration,

I cut the bonds that tied your ankles together.

With this information, Oedipus is ready to move from the mind to the body, from ambiguity to certainty. There is little need for further reasoning. What is required is merely the factual observation that

I have had the mark as long as I can remember.

The true identity between the proper name and the definite description is then brought out in the messenger's words,

That was why you were given the name you bear.

The solution to the equation is thus in the name itself. "Oedipus" means "Swollen-foot." And yet, the name retains some of the vagueness necessary for tragedy. Whereas "Oidi" translates as "swell," "Oida" means "I know." Never is this macabre play on words more effective than when the Corinthian first arrives and inquires for Oedipus. Thus, in an almost literal translation, he asks

| *Strangers, from you might I learn where* | *[oimopou]* |
| *is the palace of the Tyrannus Oedipus* | *[oidipou]* |

To be certain beyond any doubt, Oedipus checks the final details. He persists in his questioning of the man who escaped. He wants to know the number of men who killed Laios. This is now a rather futile exercise, but not entirely pointless. In contrast to Oedipus, Jocasta can no longer remain methodical. She never bothers with the determination of yet another constant. Instead she jumps immediately to the end of the proof. She cries out,

> *Ah, Miserable!*
> *That is the only word I have for you now.*
> *That is the only word I can ever have.*

She can no longer equate the name "Oedipus" with the descriptions "my King," "my husband," or "the father of my children." Only the description "Miserable" is appropriate. In the new context, anything less is false. Only words of grief are informative.

When Oedipus proceeds to the last calculations, he finds that only one man, single-handed, did the killing. Finally he is satisfied. The reasoning is correct. There is nothing more to learn. Construction by negation has run its course. Oedipus is doomed by his past. Not because any man wished it that way, but because he himself was faithful to his own logic and to his own pronouncement, even though it had been uttered in ignorance and anger. He accepts the consequences. Whether his reasoning rules had been appropriate is not for him to decide. And yet, when

Set Your Mind at Rest

ambiguity is replaced by certainty, fearful horror topples cool deliberation. He cries

> *Ah, God!*
> *It was true!*
>
> > > *All the prophecies!*
> > > > *—Now*
>
> *O Light, may I look on you for the last time!*
> *I, Oedipus,*
> *Oedipus, damned in his birth, in his marriage damned,*
> *Damned in the blood he shed with his own hand!*

It was all fate. Yet every act was free.

Courage has borne its thankless fruit. Oedipus is defeated by his own means. Nothing is to be done. The true identities must be accepted. The world has finally been anchored in the unyielding, for the unyielding is in who you are. Lives are torn apart at the moment they are brought together. So, when Jocasta recognizes what the identities are, she tries to break them by reestablishing them anew. As it is retold,

> *She ran to the apartment in her house.*
> *Her hair clutched by the fingers of both hands.*
> *She closed the doors behind her; then by that bed*
> *Where long ago the fatal son was conceived—*
> *That son who should bring about his father's death—*
> *We hear her call upon Laios, dead so many years,*
> *And heard her wail for the double fruit of her marriage,*
> *A husband by her husband, children by her child.*

In the same manner, Oedipus searches for a new identity in the old. His mind scratches for a different anchorage. Groping in his blindness for his daughters' heads, he begs

>*Could I but touch them*
>*They would be mine again, as when I had eyes.*

And yet he sees that their identity will never be complete in the same sense that his own was complete. The difference is that whereas his identities extended both into the past and into the future, theirs will be only in the past. Thus he notes,

>*Then, whom*
>*Can you ever marry? There are no bridegrooms for you,*
>*And your lives must wither away in sterile dreaming.*

Perhaps in the end, the issue is not who you are. Perhaps it is rather a matter of being or not being, for identity is itself rooted in existence. Yet, when there is nothing existing to cling to, then the mind must suffice. Only anarchists can roll with the tide and Oedipus is no anarchist. The chorus confirms by singing

>*Alas for the seed of men.*
>
>*What measure shall I give these generations*
>*That breathe on the void and are the void*
>*And exist and do not exist.*

The measure is zero. Zero is the measure of nothing. That measure belongs to the mind. It subsists, for nobody has held zero in his hands.

●

In the struggle between ultimates no one wins. Except perhaps Creon, the pretender who loves order and until the time at Colonus can make right through might. Both sides are right because both are wrong. Both are wrong because both are right. Wrestling with paradoxes is therefore the only way to learn, for genuine paradoxes can be neither solved nor ignored. And yet, when the times come, as they did for Oedipus Tyrannus, we understand what we do not understand. What is at the end was already at the beginning. Learning who Oedipus was presumably solved the problem for the city, although Sophocles never bothered to say. What he did say was that in the beginning nobody knew, and that in the end nobody rejoiced. Honesty is in pursuit and pursuit is in tragedy. Tragedy is a game watched by God, but played by men. Whatever fate there is, we bring on ourselves. To do otherwise is to be dishonest to oneself. To be dishonest is to break the rules of one's own rules. In the long run that is impossible.

Hazerdous Hazard

To translate is to express a sense in another language-parole. It is to carry
to heaven without death and to remove the dead body or remains of a
saint. It is to convey an idea from one art form to another. It is to make new
boots from the remains of old ones. It is to interpret signs.

The definitions come from the *OED*. The conclusions are my own:
Much is aVOIDable, translation is not. Anywhere/anytime, aeneymy/
anyf(r)iend.

Anyhow:
My . is made, now I must erase it. Thus, to translate is to doubly lie,
to beget by not getting at the truth. Little wonder then that all social laws
are laws of the double. More wonder that most social scientists are one-

eyed Cyclopes unable to imagine perspective; misled by our singular vision we tend to confuse use and mention, word and object.

Where is he, that wondrous wandering wonderer capable of releasing Ulysses from his wake?

●　　●　　●

In the convent, the point is more conventional:

All understanding involves crucial elements of translation, of movement from one conceptual world to another. Thus, all understanding is by necessity metaphoric, for I must always grasp what I wonder about as something different; the I becomes an Other, the Other becomes a Me.

It cannot be said more clearly:

To wonder about understanding is to be involved in language. But, to be involved in language is to exploit the distinctive connection between name and object, thing and relation, appearance and essence.

Already Odysseus, caught in the Cyclops's cave, knew that there is a distinction between what I think-and-say and what I think-and-say about. Wondering about understanding must consequently not be limited to the semantics of the signs that signify what I am talking *about*. It must also involve the pragmatics and syntax of the categorizations and relations I am talking *in*. The challenge is not to be tuned to the vibrations of my vocal chords or to detect the spots I leave on the white sheet. It is rather to be aware of the silent forces that sneak away into the emptiness that ties the marks together. But the overwhelming practice is to concentrate solely on what appears on the lines. The blank spaces that separate and unite them go unnoticed, precisely because they separate and unite.

So:

See not only what is on the lines, but also what is between them! Read less of what I am sufficiently ignorant to write and more of what you know so well that it must be passed over in silence! Deafen yourself to the noise of the expressible! Listen instead for the whisper of the taken-for-granted! But be most curious about the limits between categories, for it is only in the act of crossing a boundary that you mistranslate and consequently learn! Everything else is obedient reproduction.

●　　●　　●

Virtually everything is reproduction. But virtue is in the constraining constraints of the mimicking social sciences, vice in the liberating possibilities of the creative arts. This makes it possible to predict the future (as in Foucault's *scientia sexualis*) and impossible to presense it (as in his *ars erotica*). And yet, it is part of logic itself that 1984 is in the midst of the 1980s. I therefore write now as a way of anticipating this new world at the decade's end.

The outlines of this new world are already present, for how could it otherwise be recognized. It is a world in which the familiar industrial mode of production is overtaken by a hitherto unknown state mode of production. Although the transformation can be read off the patience cards that already lie on the table, this is not to say that the present determines the future. Rather it is often the reverse, because our hopes and fears for the future let us see only certain aspects of the present. But what is shown to the observer are merely masks. The future itself remains as invisible as the ontological stuff it is made of.

The following are nevertheless 1990-oriented questions to the 1980s:

Which aspects of the present are taboo because they are too important to reveal? Which types of legitimating unknowing is society's science in the midst of creating? How is today's state capitalism disguising its fundamental contradictions? How do I notice and then interpret the signs of the rainbow in the sky? Who understands the silent language of the taken-for-granted well enough to translate it? How can I re-member what others have forgotten and how can I forget what others de-member? Is the trancelation of relations the deconstructionist's version of Wittgenstein's throwaway ladder?

And then:

Is it too early to translate the language of state capitalism or too late to trance-end its imprisonment?

• • •

Anyone who understands me eventually recognizes these stripteasing questions as nonsensical, when he has used them—as steps—to climb up beyond them.

He must transcend these rhetorical propositions. But he will not then, as Wittgenstein suggested in *Tractatus* 6.54, see the world aright. He will instead have created another world surrounded by other limits, guarded by other silences, ruled by other emperors.

How will the rulers be dressed tomorrow?

• • •

Just as no one can fully grasp Marx's *Capital* without first having studied through and understood the whole of Hegel's *Logic,* so no one can fully understand state capitalism without first having internalized the meaning of the sign /. This sign is a symbol of relations, of the unity between identity and difference.

In conventional reasoning, relations are not denoted by a slanted line but rather by the parallel lines of the equal sign. This sign is then interpreted in the Leibnizian spirit of salva veritatae and the Russellian matter of logical atomism; a proposition is held to be both true and informative only if the equal sign is flanked by a proper name on the one side and a definite description on the other or, alternatively, by two different definite descriptions of the same object. But even though the whole point of

$$E! \, (\iota x) \, (Qx) = (\exists b) \, (x) \, [(Qx) \equiv (x = b)]$$

and

$$\cup (\iota x) \, (Qx) = (\iota b) \, \{ \, (x) \, [(Qx) \equiv (x = b)] \& (\cup b) \}$$

is to define away the definite description (ιx) (Qx), this *Principia* trick (*14.02 and *14.01) of abolishing definite descriptions by not *mentioning* them does not alter the fact that understanding requires their *use*. In use, however, definite descriptions reveal themselves as what they really are: contextual, metaphoric, and self-referential. This is in deed why Russell wanted to rid them from all analysis; in his own words, "Every proposition and every belief must have an object other than itself."

Materialists must now ask the idealist question:

Which is the object of state capitalism and its precursing postmodernism, if it has to be an object other than itself?

The emerging answer:

Perhaps there is no such object, for the major characteristic of state capitalism is that it is paradoxically locked into itself.

Next question:

How is it constructed, the self-referential reasoning net capable of catching the emerging world of masturbation?

•   •   •

By writing / instead of =, I signal my interest in dialectical, internal, and self-referential relations, names that most analysts have learned neither to use nor to mention. The words themselves are banned by the Church of Fundamentalists.

The ban was issued because all relations (including equalities) are of an ontological kind alien to the ruling ideology of presence. Thus, relations are by necessity invisible as the emptiness between the lines of my text, inaudible as the silences that turn meaningless noise into meaningful words; the untouchable is pariah, the pariah untouchable. In society's interest of communication, there is consequently a strong tendency to do away with relations by thingifying them. In this tragedy of the common, however, the interest is turned from the concept of the relation itself to the phenomena or things related. Rather than questioning the relations we are talking *in,* we stare ourselves blind on what we are talking *about.* Instead of wondering about = or /, we get caught in the sign - -. This sign is a symbol of things related.

Direct contact with / is culturally forbidden. This is why it intrigues me, for whatever is dangerous enough to be taboo is important enough to understand. The constructive is not to question the static means of representative samples but to unravel the dynamic variance of distributional tails. And yet, culture is founded on its limits, civilization on its madness.

Thus:

Relations are not only relations between measurable things but also ~~between~~ cultural words, not only words but concepts, not only concepts but meanings, not only meanings but other relations. It follows that relations are always related to other relations, all connected into strangely looping spirals. Self-reference is the word for this peculiar concept coiled at the center of current thought and extending beyond its frontiers.

Self-reference is the key to the coming revolution of the social sciences. Where are the locksmiths who know the code?

•　　•　　•

Relations like beauty, sincerity, trust, malice, disgust, and nausea are not in the things themselves but in culturally determined conceptions and behaviors; isolated things are as meaningless as connected relations are meaningful. This is why comparative studies are both so promising and so dangerous; promising because they lead to understanding of the I through the Other, dangerous because they are potentially emancipatory. Benjamin, Horkheimer, Adorno, and Marcuse all set examples. But so does everyone else who in exile experiences how one never learns home until one goes away. But each exit is an exit with no return as Homeland becomes the safe symbol of escape.

Illustrative examples are in Geertz's analyses of the Balinese cock fights. For a Western anthropologist it is easy to see those ritual dances as being performed not by roused birds but by people who via their cocks tie and untie knots of family relations. It is more difficult to interpret your reading of this writing as an integral part of the social sciences' death and initiation rites.

And yet, a rite of author(ity) is exactly what this dual relation is: Preparations for the cooking of the raw. But who knows the recipe? Who are the cooks and who are the cooked? And who furnishes the pot and the tempting spices?

• • •

The relations that tie the one to the many and the many to the one are at the same time determining culture and determined by culture.

Writing those words is easy. Reading them is incredibly difficult. The reason is that whenever I talk *about* culture I must talk *in* culture; culture is like its own language in that it is bound to use itself to understand itself. And so it is that any social scientist is handicapped by the methodological praxis that requires him to be more stupid than he actually is. Thus, in the interests of discipline, verification, and communication, he relies mainly on the two senses of sight and hearing: What counts is what can be counted; what can be counted is what can be pointed to; what can be pointed to is what can be unequivocally named. Accumulation of knowledge about the nameable is consequently the point of the scientist's game. Power, though, is not in uttering the nameable things of commodity fetishism and penis envy but in innering their symbolic condensation of relations: *Un coup de dés* played with loaded dice.

Imagine here a Foucaldian study of filth and human excrement. To see and hear the shit is barely passable. Uh! To touch it is nauseating. Woh! But smelling and tasting it penetrates so deeply into the ego itself that it is almost unthinkable. And so it is that killing a thousand people by target-seeking robots is acceptable. But killing one person with a bloody throat bite is so brutish that the thought itself takes its holder to the asylum.

• • •

The interesting is not to note obvious facts of empirical behavior. It is rather to wonder about the particular socialization processes whereby individual and society are brought together. But this is to wonder about the taboos associated with the limit between the Ego and the Other. Put differently, the issue is how you and I distinguish ourselves from each other by establishing impregnable boundaries between us.

Hazerdous Hazard

Perhaps the question is:

If definitions require distinctions, do relations affirm them by transcending them?

Or, more operationally:

How do I teach my children to tell the truth and yet realize that truth telling can sometimes be evil and therefore forbidden? How does the Family Circ(l)e turn human beings into swine?

● ● ●

Relations are often called mystical and thereby silenced. Perhaps this practice reflects the fact that proper understanding of social relations is a prerequisite for the understanding of power. But such an understanding is too fundamental for society to afford. Adam's apple is a double symbol of temptation-and-fall and of knowledge stuck in manly throats.

Power is another word for the relation between the I and the non-I. It follows that the process of liberation can never end, for its driving force is in the emancipation and creation of the self. Once this is understood, it is easier to see not only that all power involves issues of translation but also that every power struggle is a struggle of independence; power would not be power if it were not a relation, i.e., if it were not of an ontological kind different from the things in which it momentarily seeks to hide. He who has power knows how to mislead by mixing ontologies, pretending to be concerned with things while in reality knowing that things are meaningless until tied into meaningful relations. The essence of power is thus in the slanted /, its appearance in the repetitive - -.

And so it is an integral part of all relations that we tend not to notice them until they begin to malfunction. Neither do I notice the air I breathe or the blood in my veins until the relation between them is disturbed. When it is, however, then every doctor is preconditioned not to wonder about the relation per se but rather about the things of oxygen and pumping muscles; we ask not about the relation /, but about the categories - -.

In this movement from / to - -, questions of epistemology turn to questions of ontology:

Is the practice of defining our problems into existence a technique for getting at truth or for defining them away? Is it the practice of those in power to thingify relations and thereby block the road to deeper insights? Is it in society's collective interest to mislead its individuals into seeing appearance rather than essence? Are we stuck in the serpent's truth that "God knows that when you eat of the fruit of the tree in the midst of the garden your eyes will be opened and you will be like God, knowing good and evil"? Is the sign "God" nothing but the proper name of the definite description "the collective unconscious"? Is the Barefoot-Father-with-the-Beard a fetish of that social glue that is important enough to be taboo? Is the crucified son of flesh and bone merely another stage-stop on the ontological journey from subsisting relations to existing things? Is reification deification, deification reification?

Yes!

The reason for the yes is that there is no objective reality to reflect upon, for what appears is itself essentially a reflection of the reflector's subjective self-awareness of that reality. As the dialectics of flexuous flexion runs its course, questions of ontology therefore turn to self-reflective questions of mythology:

Why is the serpent the symbol of self-reference? Is it because it knows the secret of the collective unconscious?

•   •   •

When a social scientist deifies by reifying, he christens the sign - - as "society and individual." There is much to indicate that the dialectical interplay between these two categories currently is under serious strain. Perhaps the malfunctioning is most illustrative in welfare states like Sweden, where the crisis is less a matter of resources and more one of democracy. For what other is democracy than a powerful set of principles whereby one-and-many, many-and-one are forged together into what is presented as functional efficiency and moral justice? Put differently, the principles of demoncrazy shape and reflect how the psychological concept of the ego is translated into constitutional law; the high court positioned as

Hazerdous Hazard

frontier guard in the wasteland between the I and the Other, therefrom ruling over what is equal to what, over good and evil, life and death.

Some claim that the social collective now has penetrated deeply into the realm of the individual. Others note the complementary trends toward privatization. In my interpretation, these same tendencies are further indications that capitalism is in the midst of a rapid, decisive, and irreversible transformation from industrial capitalism into a form of centralized state capitalism. Both individual and society have yet to adjust to this fundamental change from one dominant production mode to another. For this to occur it is necessary to develop new decision procedures, perhaps even new personality types. Whether we like it or not, that is also the direction in which we are heading. As in the previous shift from the feudal to the capitalist mode, devils and witches are invented as scapegoats for commodity fetishists.

Who are the witches today? How is it determined whether they sink or float?

• • •

Now it can be thought-and-said:

There is time for a new Marx. This is due both to the atrocities committed in his name and to the disrepute brought by his parties to dialectics. But it is mainly because objective reality no longer is the same; as Marx himself foresaw, quantitative changes in capital have led to qualitative changes in Capital. It is obvious, for instance, that the modern suburbs of Stockholm differ drastically from Manchester a century ago not only in their outer form but also in their functioning. And yet, the sense of human deprivation inherent in the repressive domination of man by man may be just as intense now as then. Thus, the human sacrifices continue, for the gods of social cohesion and rational exchange are as demanding today as ever before. The profiteering guardian has simply changed from the suit of the old capitalist into the open shirt of the new social bureaucrat; what is inside the velour pants is nevertheless the same as was inside the strip(p)ed trousers. Perhaps most analysts were too busy trying to understand the old world to notice how the new was changing. Perhaps he who once was turned on his head now is being turned back on his feet.

The emerging / in individual/society seems most evident in the grass-roots movements currently spreading throughout the developed world. Here it is striking how the protests now focus less on the conditions of work and more on the holy family itself; it is in the micropowers of daily life at home, nursery, school, commuting, and hospital that we concretely experience the modern forms of social imprisonment. It is in those spheres of immediate existence that society reveals its fundamental contradictions of unfairness. It is through changes in familial relations that state capitalism both reveals and hides itself.

Timely questions:

Which identity crises are in the commodities of the culture industry? Who would Oedipus have been without Laios? How do you rid yourself of the superego, if the superego is not a person but a faceless collectivity? Where does it reside, the fearful authoritarianism of state capitalism?

●　　●　　●

It is easy to turn to Habermas on the ensuing crisis of legitimation. It is nevertheless more important to wonder about counterfinality, i.e., about how we came to live in a world that is opposite to the good intentions it grew out of. But counterfinality flies in the face of traditional thought, for it is a situation in which the truths of the premises have not been preserved in the conclusions. It raises the issue of how I tell truths about a world whose very nature it is to be a lie:

What reasoning tools do I employ when I realize that the social world does not obey the rules of conventional truth-functional logic? What do I do when I notice that state capitalism has many traits in common with such enemies of our culture as paradox and tragedy? Who is to blame when everything is perfectly right in the beginning and everything horribly wrong in the end?

No one is to blame, for no one has broken those behavioral rules of reasoning into which she has been socialized. The tragic hero as expression of the Eros of the Western ethos!

So:

How are we socialized into thinking-and-acting in ways that are at the same time individually praiseworthy and in the interest of society's state capitalism? How do I move from categorizing crosses and directional arrows to self-referential loops? How do people learn to live in institutionalized double bind without going crazy?

•　•　•

The transformation of industrial capitalism into state capitalism is already evident in the socialization and reproduction processes whereby society and individual are being adjusted to each other. By fulfilling moral codes, we experience how the temptation to dream and transform is overcome. But to experience is not to understand, even though it is a necessary step toward that boundary between the I and the Other where understanding resides. This boundary is taboo, now as much as in Paradise itself. In the process of trespassing, the anxiety of relations is turned into the fear of things, issues of power into fig leaves. And yet, castration is the metaphor that (fe)male power seems most eager to suppress.

So:

How can I simultaneously anchor - - in / and / in - -? If I ever did, how would I then translate my insights into communicable expressions without destroying them? How can you and I as individuals eavesdrop on society when it thinks-and-talks about itself in-through itself? How do I capture the dialectic of society and individual without falling into the - - trap of sociology and psychoanalysis?

•　•　•

Caught in culture, the only way to produce is to re-produce by putting words out of conventional contexts, by making new boots from the remains of old ones. Thus it is in self-reflection that reason sees its own interest. To ask again is consequently not to repeat but to translate anew.

Therefore:

Which forces of social cohesion are illustrated and further entrenched in the Odyssean act of ontological juggling? Is his appearance essential or is his function merely to divert attention from the pickpockets that raid the applauding audience? How is this desiring piece of writing itself a legitimating instance of the socialization processes of state capitalism? Is not striptease the appropriate metaphor of a society that talks about its own silences, reveals the powers it exerts, and promises to rid itself of the laws that protect it?

What does it mean to engage in dialectically mediating history-specific communication?

● ● ●

The challenge is enormous. Not for the well-ordered disciplines of the social sciences, but for their individual members exploring the limits of culture. Mallarmé was eons ahead:

NOTHING WILL HAVE TAKEN PLACE EXCEPT THE PLACE

EXEPTÉ

PEUT-ÊTRE

UNE CONSTELLATION

Toute Pensée émet un Coup de Dés

Hazerdous hazard.

Social Space of Silence

Everyone knows that I talk very little. But at certain times I was driven to talk by a force so compelling, I felt determined to transform the most simple details of life into so many insignificant words, that my voice, which was becoming the only space where I allowed her to live, forced her to emerge from her silence too, and gave her a sort of physical certainty, a physical solidity, which she would not have had otherwise.

Maurice Blanchot, Death Sentence, p. 73

●

The challenge is enormous. Not for the well-ordered disciplines of the social sciences, but for their individual members exploring the limits of culture. Mallarmé was eons ahead:

NOTHING WILL HAVE TAKEN PLACE EXCEPT THE PLACE

EXEPTÉ

PEUT-ÊTRE

UNE CONSTELLATION

Toute Pensée émet un Coup de Dés

Hazerdous hazard

•

"There's glory for you!"
"I don't know what you mean by 'glory' ", Alice said.
Humpty Dumpty smiled contemptuously. "Of course you don't—till I tell you. I meant 'there's a nice knock-down argument for you' ".
"But 'glory' doesn't mean 'a nice knock-down argument' ", Alice objected.
"When I use a word", Humpty Dumpty said in a rather scornful tone, "it means just what I choose it to mean—neither more nor less".
"The question is", said Alice, "whether you can make words mean so many different things".
"The question is", said Humpty Dumpty, "which is to be master—that's all".

Lewis Carrol, *The Annotated Alice,* pp. 268–69

Social Space of Silence

• • •

Questions spring from the constellation of quotes: WHAT IS THE
DIFFERENCE BETWEEN YOU AND ME?

Rephrased and operationalized: Which difference makes a difference?
What is an ontological transformation? How is touchable turned into
untouchable, sound into silence, letter into meaning? Is power the power of
meaning, meaning the meaning of power?

Is the power to produce meaning with the repres(s)entative editor,
proudly appointed by society to guard and to legitimate the right to write? Is
it with the creative writer, publicly relieving himself on sheets of paper? Is it
with the responsive reader, privately experiencing anew what she already
knew? Put differently: Is power in the authority of the author or in the
auditing of the audience? Or is power at the same time everywhere and
nowhere, always evasive yet in every glance, every touch, every mouth?

For answers, take your analytic prick, s'il vous plaît: Un oeuf à la
Descartes in the elegant Bar de Saussure? Or some scrambled Humpties
from the basement of Alice's Restaurant? The personal touch of the French
or the common sense of Anglo-America? Remember, though, that the
philosopher himself always had breakfast on eggs hatched for eight to ten
days. Lonely babe in Babylone staring through his whoroscope.

"Damn it all! Can't have a paper without words, you know!" Which
was Lord Peter Wimsey's way of saying that the language of power is in the
power of language, the power of language in the language of power. No
exit, for the phenomenon I wish to write *about* is at the same time the
medium I am forced to write *within*. Once again caught in the familiar
chains of self-reference, telling truths about lies and lies about truths.
Confined within the prison house of communication, what I happen to say is
not what *I* want to say but what the *saying* wants to say. All criticism is by
necessity an exercise in metalanguage, all learning a struggle with paradox.
Start talking with your cell mate, Epimenides!

It is in this paradoxical sense of foreclosure that language is both its
own problem and its own solution; since I cannot mention a word without
using it, every negation is predicated on a form of affirmation. Perhaps this
is why Penelope locked herself up with her tapestry woven at dawn and

undone at dusk: activity for activity's sake; time for time; weaving not for the web but for the weaving of the web. The evasive principles of deconstruction had no doubt been in Ithaca, Greece, long before they reached Paris, Baltimore, New Haven, and Ithaca, New York. Shadows reflecting.

●

Simultaneously evasive and aggressive, most postmodernists tend to be explicitly self-conscious. Every discourse is by them held to be heterogeneous, every meaning to embody the structure of undecidability, every text to be contextual. The only way to grasp and break out of such a reality is to perform radical experiments, for to *ex-periment* means literally to go outside limits, to refuse accepted categories, to fight codification. There is no alternative, for in categories lies the status quo of conservatism, in codes the totalitarianism of the norm(al).

It is as textual experiments that language approaches solutions to its own problems. The reason is that every utterance contains a crucial element of persuasion; there is no truth without opinion, no description without performance. Telling truths or lies is consequently not enough. Being convincing is equally necessary and that is regardless of whether the text in question is a theorem, a scientific paper, a novel, a poem, or anything else. The urge to express is linked with the urge to impress, the grasping of meaning with the evocation of meaning. Logic and rhetoric reach for one another. So do ethics and aesthetics.

As an integral part of the crisis of realism, there is fiction in every truth, truth in every fiction. And thus it is that Marcel Duchamp had no choice but to strip his bride bare, for new truths require new categories, new chattergories new forms of authority. But a comment on a text is itself a text. Etymology indeed suggests that to write a text is to weave a texture of words, to produce a ready-made tissue for blowing your nose or for wiping your ass. Is reading and writing a kind of anal erotics, a symbol of subject and object united? Who is to be master-baitor? That's all.

The analyst asks: Is the meaning of such critical texts in your reading from the outside or in my writing from the inside? Is reading a search for

Social Space of Silence

knowledge, writing a mode of action? Is textual power in the inferential logic of factual reference or in the productive rhetoric of speech acts? Is the locus of power in the things denoted or in the words denoting? Where *is* the difference?

The questions prompt themselves. For it is in the theory and practice of current literature that language simultaneously reflects reality and constitutes it. If this is correct, then it must be explicitly recognized that every discourse has the potential both for manipulation and for evasion; every statement holds back and sets free at the same time. Does it follow that the power of words lies not in their users directly but in the social relations that knot them together? Is power in the abcdef-mindedness of rhythmic expressions? Is power a tautology anchored in conventional rules of inference? Are external and internal hiding behind the same veil of being? Is it there that ontologies are transformed?

Modern theories often imply that the power of words lies in other words. Signs are thought to embrace other signs. Signs copulate. Signs materialize. Word turns to body, body to word, and eventually into a marching army of metaphors, metonymies, and anthropomorfeces. As a consequence, there has been a movement beyond the theoretical realms of logic and dialectics into the practice of rhetoric: Possessing a language is for understanding and speaking alike.

Living with such a double possession is to experience how the present is always past, the past always present. In the here-and-now midst of the ruling metaphysics of presence, there is in fact a language of radical absence, for words never denote directly, always indirectly. A word is never the thing itself, merely a version thereof. It is nevertheless in their desire for presence that words take on some thinglike properties, partly as a function of the mythological tendency to reify denotation, partly as a reflection of phonology and the anagrammatic nature of letters. The alienation produced by these tendencies is not social or psychological but profoundly ontological. The conclusion stems from Jacques Derrida: Difference deferred is a difference that makes a difference. *Différance* is the term to deread a gain from.

Despite the current fashion of analytico-referential historiography and biography, it may therefore be writers like Nietzsche, Kafka, Musil, Blanchot, and Barthes that come closest to the evasive spirit of the present. It is within the fragmentary and aphoristic works of these authors that they allow the precision of ambiguity to rule over the vagaries of the historically specific. Employing such techniques, they manage to write both *in* and *of* power, to grasp ontological transformations in their process of transformation, to realize that tautology is a frozen state of reasoning and that concentration camps represent a degenerate form of power. Thus it is in the struggle with self-reference that both reader and writer are first caught in a maze of old cross-references and then asked to participate in the production of new meanings. Yet, the value of such texts is less in the hinted answers and more in the unknown questions. It is in fact in the tradition of deconstruction to aim for the unanswerable, not to affirm the positive but to reflect the negative; what is thereby destroyed is not meaning per se but the unequivocal domination of one meaning over all others.

Therefore: Insult the wor(l)d and it will reveal the taboos of the social space of silence! In everyday speech, language is idling. In avant-garde literature, it works at a pitch, experimenting with the intelligibilities of today's text. It is in the crevice between convention and deviance that language becomes erotic.

●　　●　　●

One way to fight the totalitarianism of codification is always to begin anew. Another is to write in fragments. Since the lover's relation to the loved one is of an extreme solitude, these were also the approaches that Roland Barthes used in his moving book *A Lover's Discourse.* Like its own subject matter, this discourse does not set out to realize a small number of well-defined wishes. Instead, it merely moves on, continuously and unpredictably new, guided by nothing but the randomness of alphabetese. Form and content are here brought together in a play of ambiguity, paradox, and irony. The hope is not to capture human relations in the nets of descriptive sociology, but to let them free in subversive action. SO IT IS A LOVER WHO SPEAKS AND WHO SAYS: Never bide your turn, never worry about the future. And so it comes that Barthes's quote from Tao can serve as its own verification: "He does not show himself and shines. He does not affirm himself and prevails. His work done, he does not attach himself to it, his work will remain" (Roland Barthes, *A Lover's Discourse,* p. 233).

Ready?

Can't stop them now. Here they come. Three words. Two empty spaces in between: I LOVE YOU.

Noun of love. Verb of love. Present tense. Action word doubly embraced. Subject and object linked together. First person reaching out for a second. Thus it is that when I say I LOVE YOU, I do not denote but perform. Whenever I repeat the banal words, I do not participate in an explanatory sermon but in the chanting of a hymn. I do not analyze but confess. My utterance lacks content, yet is full of meanings. As a tautological amen, it is a cry at the outer limits of language. It tells nothing but confirms everything. High above the crowd, Chagall's blue bride throws herself from one trapeze to another, floating in air, unquestioning, yet driven by an intense curiosity, reaching for the outstretched hands. No one understands, because the lover's discourse is so exceedingly solitary, itself a reflection of a loneliness that is not psychological but systemic.

Barthes's nontotalitarian epistemology has a formal counterpart in his use of pronouns and tenses. The he, she, it of the thingified third person are taken over by the I and you of the first and the second. The past *was* is replaced by the present *is.* As if to prove itself, love in fact turns into jealousy exactly at that moment when the persons of you and me are erased by the things of him or her; the ungraspable is destroyed exactly when its symbols are impoverished into material signifiers; torn by jealousy, the loved one remembers the simplicity of physical details and forgets the richness of total relations. What is grasped is the body not the spirit of the letter. What is lost is the insight that desire issues from lack not from presence; absence is transformed into an ordeal of abandonment.

Prior to that moment of alienation, however, I ask not with my mouth but with my eyes. I answer not with words but with glances. Love sees clearly. Love is not blind. Like Molly Bloom in the cool of the evening, I therefore ask you with my eyes to ask again. Yes, my mountain flower. And I put my arms around you, thereby proving that, whenever in doubt, the body becomes the word's corrective. The hell with the telephone! For "with my language I can do everything: even and especially *say nothing*. I can do everything with my language, *but not with my body.* What I hide by my language, my body utters. I can deliberately mold my message, not my voice. By my voice, whatever it says, the other will recognize 'that something is wrong with me'. I am a liar (by preterition), not an actor. My body is a stubborn child, my language is a very civilized adult" (Roland Barthes, *A Lover's Discourse,* pp. 43–44).

Like a stubborn child, love is not a conversationist. All it does is in effect to mumble to itself, far removed from the pursuit of compromise. Monologue is therefore the language form that best reflects the fact that the lover never resigns, never waits in line, never fights about the final word, never wrinkles his forehead, never shakes his fist. All he does is to laugh and cry. Not as a concerned sociologist or a powerful politician. But as the liberating artist he happens to be.

And thus. In the fantastic banalities of love I desire not *what* you are but *that* you are, not fetishized things but untouchable relations. Ecstasy and stillness come together in the moment that I love you, so you love yourself. It is you I want, you⠀⠀⠀⠀⠀⠀and in you myself. In the loving calm of your arms I become two in one, motherhood and sexuality united. And "her brother's body pressed so tenderly, so sweetly against her, that she felt she was resting within him as he in her; nothing in her stirred her now, even her splendid desire" (Robert Musil, *The Man without Qualities,* as quoted in Roland Barthes, *A Lover's Discourse,* p. 224).

At that rare moment of perfect communication, the enchantment is turned into the bliss impossible to name. And whereof one cannot speak, thereof one must be silent. The unspeakable is the mystical, the mystical beyond the limits. It is from that empty space on the other side that I hear echoes of the banal chants. I LOVE YOU. "Und alles, was man weiss, nicht bloss, rauschen und brausen gehört hat, lässt sich in drei Worten sagen" (Ludwig Wittgenstein, *Tractatus Logico-Philosophicus,* dedication page).

•

In his final works Roland Barthes staged an utterance, not an analysis. The discourse is used, not reduced; shown, not said. A glimpse of nakedness. A fold in the velvet gown suggests that "language is a skin: I rub my language against the other. It is as if I had words instead of fingers, or fingers at the tip of my words. My language trembles with desire. The emotion derives from a double contact: on the one hand, a whole activity of discourse discreetly, indirectly focuses upon a single signified which is "I desire you" and releases, nourishes, ramifies it to the point of explosion (language experiences orgasm upon touching itself); on the other hand, I enwrap the other in my words, I caress, brush against, talk up this contact, I extend myself to make the commentary to which I submit the relation endure" (Roland Barthes, *A Lover's Discourse,* p. 73).

• • •

Shocking discovery! Imagine. All your work made of words. Of words alone. "It is as though you had discovered that your wife were made of rubber: the bliss of all those years, the fears . . . from sponge. It's worse than discovering your privates are plastic" (William H. Gass, *Fiction and the Figures of Life,* pp. 27–28). Is that where power resides? In the plastic? In the rubber? In the physicality of the words themselves?

In deed. Touch the wordy world! Hold it in your hand! Caress it! Squeeze it! Move it to your tender fingertips! And it will come. From the depths of the unconscious well waves of meaningful images. It is in this type of relation that most writers stand to their words. No wonder, then, that language means so much. For to us, the late surrealists, language is like a lover, "not the language of love, but the love of language, not matter, but meaning, not what the tongue touches, but what it forms, not lips and nipples, but nouns and verbs" (William H. Gass, *On Being Blue,* p. 11). The geographic inference problem of 1968 dressed up in the garb of 1984. Oh well! Ready maid.

But even though expressions are immediately physical, they have a nonphysical side as well. Marx called one of these sides use value and the other exchange value; Frege termed them reference and sense, Saussure signifier and signified, Austin brute and institutional facts, Derrida presence and absence. In general, preference is given to the first term in these pairs of difference. But to have power is to know how one face is turned into the other, to exhibit the visible and profit on the invisible, to whitewash with the transparent and color with the opaque. Power is always in the quest of security, in attempts to freeze the future.

It is nevertheless in the back rooms of the Bar de Saussure that commodities can be heard speaking directly to one another. After the tiniest sip of analysis, they begin to reveal their trade secret: "Our use value may be a thing that interests men. It is no part of us as objects. What, however, does belong to us as objects is our value. Our natural intercourse as commodities proves it. In the eyes of each other, we are nothing but exchange values" (Karl Marx, *Capital,* vol. 1, p. 83). The same holds for expressions in general, including money and other promissory notes. In the process, rites of mythology are metamorphosed into laws of State, raw into cooked, cooked into cocked.

When this general power strategy is carried to extremes, the visible is overemphasized and the invisible left in darkness. What is repressed is the nonrepres(s)entable other. The effect is growing alienation of the type that Marx illustrated in his discussion of fetishism, and Lacan exemplified in his theory of castration. What counts are countable things. What is taboo are totemic relations. Foucault later drew attention to the same forces of reification through his remark that current ideology highlights the *scientia sexualis* and hides the *ars erotica;* there is a parallel in the development of his own writings from the history of madness to the history of sexuality. In the game of ontological transformations, the flipper is always a touch ahead.

Like the double-faced Janus, the flip-flopper knows how to join contradictions without going crazy. Perhaps it is therefore Janus, the janitor, who is the incarnation of modern power. Perhaps it is the priests of his congregation who know how to detect the difference between you and me. Perhaps it is they who separate the wheat from the chaff and who single out those traces of the past that are let through the Now-gate into the future.

But wait! Janus has a distant relative. Dionysus! Is it rather he who is the god of power? Proper question! For like the theory of expression itself,

Dionysus is always caught in between, always dangling in the abyss between order and chaos. There is something to be re(a)d off his sheets. Is it the drops of blood from a sacrificial meal? Or just some wine spilled in an orgy? Neither, of course! Merely a piece of rhetoric to show how the intellectual's pen is his spear, the rubber his shield. Double entry, double protection. Castrated from the outset.

The différance? Repressing the represented or presenting the repressed? Why do some prefer the pleasures of ideology and others the ideologies of pleasure? But this is neither a Foucaldian pipe nor a Freudian cigar. This is this is this. What I write I write. What is a text.

•

Thus: "I have lost silence, and the regret I feel over that is immeasurable. I cannot describe the pain that invades a man once he has begun to speak. It is a motionless pain, that is itself pledged to muteness; because of it, the unbreathable is the element I breathe. I have shut myself up in a room, alone, there is no one in the house, almost no one outside, but this solitude has itself begun to speak, and I must in turn speak about this speaking solitude, not in derision, but because a greater solitude hovers above it, and above that solitude, another still greater, and each, taking the spoken word in order to smother it and silence it, instead echoes it to infinity, and infinity becomes an echo" (Maurice Blanchot, *Death Sentence,* p. 33).

It follows that tracing a text back to its experiential, referential, or intentional roots is an infinite task, a rhythmic choir humming in an ecco chamber. There is no presentation without representation, no representation without presentation. When a text speaks about itself, it therefore speaks about the world, for all that can be said is in the saying; with Lacan, the unconscious is structured like a language, a symbolic reflection of imaginary differences that make a real difference. Whatever I do and whatever I don't, I am inevitably placed within sets of complex power relations, of meanings and distinctions. As a consequence, there is a politics of texts, of readers, writers, and expressions. Which is not to say, however, that all texts are political or that all life is art, merely to suggest that the term "political" should be understood in its deeper meaning, "as describing the whole of human relations in their real, social structure, in their power of making the world; one must above all give an active role to prefix *de-;* here it represents an operational movement, it permanently embodies a defaulting" (Roland Barthes, *Mythologies,* p. 143).

It is now well recognized that modern power arrangements are doubly dependent on the concept of difference, i.e., on the interplay of presence and absence. Society's need to normalize the deviant legitimizes the use of disciplinary techniques, while being different offers the individual a way of escaping them. Power and resistance thus require each other, just as a power of separation necessitates a separation of power. Through the operation of such a dialectic of opposition, even the most critical discourse becomes an integral part of what it aims to subvert; like its own language, power is constituted by the differences it seeks to overcome. Paradoxically self-reflecting, "power is tolerable only on condition that it mask a substantial part of itself" (Michel Foucault, *The History of Sexuality,* vol. 1, p. 86).

What is masked is the insight that power is an exercise in ontological transformations. Once that veil is torn away, even the tragedy of Marxism becomes intelligible. Thus it is in reading Hegel, Marx, Kierkegaard, and Nietzsche together that it becomes clear how history turns into hypothesis, hypothesis into thesis, thesis into norm, norm into counterfinality. Emerging as a critical issue is not the comparison of one utopia with another, but the social function of utopian thought itself. The reason is that "*utopias* afford consolation: although they have no real locality there is nevertheless a fantastic, untroubled region in which they are able to unfold; they open up cities with vast avenues, superbly planted gardens, countries where life is easy, even though the road to them is chimerical. *Heterotopias* are disturbing, probably because they secretly undermine language, because they make it impossible to name this *and* that, because they shatter or tangle common names, because they destroy "syntax" in advance, and not only the syntax with which we construct sentences but also that less apparent syntax which causes words and things (next to and also opposite one another) to "hold together". This is why utopias permit fables and discourse: they run with the very grain of language and are part of the fundamental dimension of the *fabula;* heterotopias (such as those to be found so often in Borges) desiccate speech, stop words in their tracks, contest the very possibility of grammar at its source; they dissolve our myths and sterilize the lyricism of our sentences (Michel Foucault, *The Order of Things,* p. xviii).

•

Stopping words in their tracks is to engage in ideology critique, to make silence speak. Ideology is in fact sometimes defined as the totality of that which goes without saying, as that taken-for-granted which is so transparent that it casts neither reflection nor shadow. But even though most secrets dwell in the whiteness of degree zero, some are in the words themselves. This holds especially for the case of prefixes.

What a word, that word! Nice and naked. PREFIX. Emperor without clothes. Form and content finally united. For to *pre-fix* is to fix in advance, to fasten and to castrate. As if to stress its own self-reference, the term itself contains a prefix; it does not refer to what it is, it is what it refers to.

The most important prefixes are *re-, pre-,* and *pro-;* in the *OED,* words with these beginnings take up an amazing total of 617 pages! Although not all of these constellations actually serve as prefixes, many of them lead directly to rewarding propositions about ideological preferences. Their function is to position meaning, less in time and more in figurative space. Even though *re-* holds a privileged position, the three are intimately related. As a consequence, they cannot be analyzed one at a time but should be engaged in a free play with one another. There is a choreography of meaning, a dance of rhetorical reference.

This proposal of how to proceed reflects an epistemological premise. The presumption is that severing relations is to produce a picture of stale predilections rather than an image of living prospects. Recalling the proposals of Lacan, Barthes, and Foucault, splitting relations is in reality a procedure for masking: unrevealed tautologies are thereby called truths, not remedial prescriptions. While truth for Descartes is in the reassuring certitude of representation, for Nietzsche it is in the revolting ambiguity of the taken-for-granted. In practice, though, every preacher realizes that every premise contains a promise of predictable results, just as every promise contains a premise of profitable returns. In the process, products are reproduced, presentations represented, representations repressed. The repressed is indeed recaptured by the words themselves; the traumatic *re-* leads to the procreative *pre-*. All research searches back to the pregiven of its own initials: GO, professor, GO!

In this rerendering, progressive social science reemerges as a problematic program for the reinterpretation and subsequent representation of reality as it now presents itself. Likewise, representative democracy reappears as a procedure for reproducing remarkably representative protégés, ready to proclaim the regrettable prospects of the predominant ideology of presence. Why does proper reasoning preserve the truth of its premises in the predictions of its conclusions? Why does science retain its mythological belief in spiritual conception, regardless of the recognition that every representation is itself a presentation, every presentation itself a representation? Is the Virgin Mary the saint of reasoning? Is the Devil of rhetoric its pre-Adamic seducer?

Weave Mary! Weave! Remember the members dismembered.

•

A text about you and me. A discourse on differance. A show of ontological transformations. A premediated refrain of pronouns and proverbs. A play on the power of silence and the silence of power. A touch of metaphors. A dance of ready maids descending a staircase. An approach to limits. This is what this is.

And thus spoke Zarathustra: "I want to speak to the despisers of the body. I would not have them learn and teach differently, but merely have them say farewell to their own bodies—and thus become silent. But it is the child who says: 'Body and soul am I.' And why should one not speak like a child? [Yet] you say 'I' and you are proud of this word. But greater than this—although you will not believe in it—is your body, which does not say 'I' but performs 'I' " (Friedrich Nietzsche, *Thus Spoke Zarathustra,* my translation).

And yet. The smallest little child will soon discover that when the I is turned upside down, it still remains an I. When laid to rest, however, it becomes a dash—a mark of thought before a thought. But the same child will also learn that when a halo dot is placed above its head, the I loses its capital importance and becomes a small i. And a small i turned upside down is nothing less than an exclamation mark! The sign of infinity, though, is neither the dashing sleeping I nor the tilted relation /, but a lying 8, too tired of memories ever to stand erect again. In the meantime, the symbol -/- retains its power, for it signifies the practice of slash and burn. By no coincidence, it also happens that a slash is a slit made in a garment in order to expose to view a lining or undergarment of a different color.

Striptease as epistemology. Epistemology as striptease. Body relieved.

•   •   •

Accidentally, Werther's finger touches Charlotte's, their feet, under the table, happen to brush against each other. Werther might be engrossed by the meaning of these accidents; he might concentrate physically on these slight zones of contact and delight in this fragment of inert finger or foot, fetishistically, without concern for the response (like God—as the etymology of the word tells us—the fetish does not reply). But in fact Werther is not perverse, he is in love: he creates meaning, always and everywhere, out of nothing, and it is meaning which thrills him: he is in the crucible of meaning. Every contact, for the lover, raises the question of an answer: the skin is asked to reply.

(A squeeze of the hand—enormous documentation—a tiny gesture within the palm, a knee which doesn't move away, an arm extended, as if quite naturally, along the back of a sofa

and against which the other's head gradually comes to rest—
this is the paradisiac realm of subtle and clandestine signs: a
kind of festival not of the senses but of meaning.)
            (Roland Barthes, A Lover's Discourse, *p. 67)*

Last night, as I was sleeping, I dreamt—marvellous error!—that a spring was breaking out in my heart. I said: Along which secret aqueduct, oh water, are you coming to me, water of a new life that I have never drunk?

Last night, as I was sleeping, I dreamt—marvellous error!—that I hide a beehive here inside my heart. And the golden bees were making combs and sweet honey from my old failures.

Is my soul asleep? Have those beehives that labor at night stopped? And the water wheel of thought, is it dry, the cups empty, wheeling, carrying only shadows?

No, my soul is not asleep. It is awake. It neither sleeps nor dreams, but watches, its clear eyes open, far-off things, and listens at the shores of the great silence. (Antonio Machado, Times Alone, *pp. 42–45)*

Social Space of Silence

The Eye and the Index Finger

"Cum ipsi (majores homines) appellabant rem aliquam, et cum secundum eam vocem corpus ad aliquid movebant, videbam, et tenebam hoc ab eis vocari rem illam, quod sonabant, cum eam vellent ostendere. Hoc autem eos velle ex motu corporis aperiebatur: tamquam verbis naturalibus omnium gentium, quae fiunt vultu et nutu oculorum, ceterorumque membrorum actu, et sonitu vocis indicante affectionem animi et petendis, habendis, rejiciendis, fugiendisve rebus. Ita verba in variis sententiis locis suis posita, et crebro audita, quarum rerum signa essent, paulatim colligebam, measque jam voluntates, edomito in eis signis ore, per haec enuntiabam.

(Augustine, *Confessions,* I, 8)."[1]

---

1.   "When they [my elders] named some object, and accordingly moved towards something, I saw this and grasped that the thing was called by the

The Eye and the Index Finger

Thus begins the first paragraph of Wittgenstein's *Philosophical Investigations*. A quote. A launching pad. A germ of reformulation. An instance of intertextuality. To write is to walk on a pavement of citations.

As a way of showing my desire, I now enter the stage. Silence. A glance catches another. An index finger pins each and everyone down. You. You. You. You. You. You. You. A mouth opens. Out it comes:

"One."

    "Two."

        "Three."

            "Four."

                "Five."

                    "Six."

And then?

You fill in by silently saying "Seven." Not because "seven" is a holey number, but because it comes next in the hierarchy of the Order of Numbering. Automatically you extend my writing voice and pointing finger into the rules of counting. Without thinking, you project an individual body into collective meaning.

This is the nature of the word "seven": to be parasitic on whatever went before. In shared activities like seeing/pointing/speaking/hearing/reading/writing, we become extensions of one another; no body is a self-sufficient entity onto itself, but always a double in need of the other. What I left absent by the question "and then?" you made present by replying "seven." In my words you detected a structure of an already-but-not-yet, of

---

sound they uttered when they meant to point it out. Their intention was shewn by their bodily movements, as it were the natural language of all peoples: the expression of the face, the play of the eyes, the movement of other parts of the body, and the tone of voice which expresses our state of mind in seeking, having, rejecting, or avoiding something. Thus, as I heard words repeatedly used in their proper places in various sentences, I gradually learnt to understand what objects they signified; and after I had trained my mouth to form these signs, I used them to express my own desires" (Ludwig Wittgenstein, *Philosophical Investigations*, 1).

a project to be continued. The taken-for-granted is like Flaubert's God in the Universe: present everywhere, visible nowhere.

It is in such invisible structures that we find both the necessity and the possibility of a social and human science: in the name of reflexivity, the *pre*-sented is *re*-presented; the *re*-presented, *pre*-sented. More specifically, our study objects behave predictably because they reflect what is taken to count, just as our conclusions become predictable because they reflect the taken-for-granted of counting. In neither case, however, is this predictability intentional. On the contrary. For, as Wittgenstein put it: *"This is how it strikes me. When I obey a rule [like the rule of counting], I do not choose. I obey the rule blindly."*[2]

Put differently, I learn the meaning of a word by using it as other people do. To obey a rule is consequently a social practice, impossible to engage in privately; "to think one is obeying a rule is not to obey a rule."[3] Obeying a rule is rather a matter of participating in the routinized rituals of day-to-day life, of being socialized into accepting the normal and deploring the different. Unwittingly trained to follow orders, we get rewarded by soft words and punished by hard sticks. Ruler as ruler.

To repeat: "Learning the meaning of a word is to embrace the normal." Even a blind person can see that. Even a mute person can tell that. The question is whether you and I are deaf enough to hear it. Yet it is a well-established principle of epistemology that I understand the form and function of a particular rule only when I extend it to its logical and existential limits. Once there, I can remain forever confined or I can try to break loose. From the outside, I am then supposed to review the previously accepted, to transcend the old and create the new. To inquire about society's taken-for-granted is to call its bluff.

Moving from one categorial realm to another is to participate in a revolution. One set of takens-for-granted is replaced by another. Turning one ideology on its head, I put another on its feet. Bottoms up. Underpants. The logical positivist becomes a dialectical materialist, the realist a

---

2.   *Philosophical Investigations*, 219.
3.   *Philosophical Investigations*, 202.

The Eye and the Index Finger

surrealist, the Christian an atheist. Such Kierkegaardian leaps from one rule(r) to another are incredibly demanding, not the least because they require that one form of life be replaced by another. It is not enough to think differently. I must behave accordingly. Other clothes, other food, other friends. Other gods. All falls together in coherence, for world and life are one.

To me however, this type of conversion is not challenging enough. The reason is that I take understanding not to be in the crossing of boundaries but rather in staying right *at* them. Every experience occurs on the border, for at the center everything is so natural that it goes unnoticed. To be *at* a limit is consequently to have moved from the acceptability of the taken-for-granted to the forbidden of the taboo. To be suspended in that position is to hang in the crevice between categories, to refuse the security of being caught. Rebel instead of revolutionary.

To assume such a position is to cause a serious threat, for the acceptance of a limit is the foundation of social cohesion. As a consequence, various strategies have evolved to repress it, including the normative activities of logic, religion, and social psychology.[4] But why would a certain behavior be taboo, if it were not too dangerous to be practiced? Is the answer in Wittgenstein's conclusion that "the subject does not belong to the world: rather it is a *limit* of the world"?[5] Thus, "there is no such thing as the subject that thinks or entertains idea. [For] if I wrote a book called *The World as I found it,* I should have to include a report on my body . . . this being a method of isolating the subject . . . [But] it alone could *not* be mentioned in that book."[6] Yet it eventually turns out that this solipsistic

---

4.   Witness, for instance, Kristeva's remark that "the most profound crises of rationality, which are in this way dynamically organized, are accompanied by a rigid investiture of other archaic and repressive structures, when and if their attempts at becoming semiotic-symbolic fail. These archaic and repressive structures include order, the family, normalcy, normative classical psychological-tending discourse, all of which are just so many characteristics of fascist ideology. Consequently, we may conclude that texts on experiencing limits—this is modern art—constitute the most direct and risky approach to the fascist phenomenon" (Julia Kristeva, *The Speaking Subject,* p. 220).
5.   Ludwig Wittgenstein, *Tractatus Logico-Philosophicus,* 5.632, emphasis added.
6.   *Tractatus,* 5.631.

viewpoint coincides with pure realism, for "whatever we see could be other than it is. There is no *a priori* order of things."[7] Perhaps it is such that "language is a labyrinth of paths. You approach from *one* side and know your way about: you approach the same place from another side and no longer know your way about."[8]

There is in deed unity, not only between the young and the mature Marx but also between the early and the late Wittgenstein. What ties them together is their common struggle with issues of identity and existence, certainty and ambiguity. The focus is on the relation between I and the other. How could it be otherwise? For the paradox of (post)modernity is the paradox of the liar. Context is pervasive.

Out of these quotations grows a host of therapeutic questions: If the subject is a limit of the world, what then is a limit of the subject? The body, not to be mentioned!? What is a physical and cultural limit of the body? The skin, not to be touched!? Is the skin a bodily metaphor for the culturally taboo of limits? Is the concept of limit too dangerous to know not because it is constitutive of the subject but because it is constitutive of truth? Is this why Plato and Saint Augustine insisted that poetry and theater present the preeminent threat to truth?

Perhaps. For it is a characteristic of every theory of truth that it obeys some specific principals of law and order. At the same time, it is a major function of art to question these rule(r)s of blind obedience. This usually takes the form of experimenting with the relations between a private or inner act of meaning on the one hand and the collective or outer meaning on the other. Perhaps it is here that solipsism and realism turn into one

---

7. *Tractatus*, 5.634.
8. *Philosophical Investigations*, 203.

another, where you and I come together. What is at stake is nothing less than the creation of new cultural meanings out of old bodily forms. Revelation. But in logic there can never be surprises, for "logic is not a field in which *we* express what we wish with the help of signs, but rather one in which the nature of the natural and inevitable sign speaks for itself. If we know the logical syntax of any sign-language, then we have already been given all the propositions of logic."[9]

The paradox is that to create new meanings is to break the hitherto taken-for-granted, i.e., to violate the tautologies of connectives. But this means that I simultaneously must follow a rule and stretch the skin of its boundary. Here lies temporary madness. For "if I were sometime to see quite new surroundings from my window instead of the long familiar ones, if things, humans and animals were to behave as they never did before, then I should say something like 'I have gone mad'; but that would merely be an expression of giving up the attempt to know my way about."[10]

In short: If I am not like you, I am lost. Whenever I encounter the unexpected I have no bearings, no rules to follow, no fixes to keep me steady. Yet, the I is never altogether an I, for the I is always unfinished.

To be lost is not merely a matter of geography. It is also to be morally and socially condemned. Get lost you bastard, son of a bitch, fruit of unholy intercourse, consequence of category mixing! But a mule is a reliable worker.

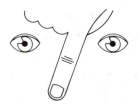

In the spirit of mixing categories, I shall now return to my opening scene. What I did there was to rely on my eyes and index finger as bodily means for looking and pointing. At the same time, I asked you to imagine

9.   *Tractatus,* 6.124.
10.   Ludwig Wittgenstein, *Zettel,* p. 393.

that sounds came out of my mouth, while in fact marks came out of my pen:

"One."

    "Two."

        "Three."

            "Four."

                "Five."

                    "Six."

And then I presumed that you behaved normally by saying "Seven." Nothing unusual. In doubt, ask your anaesthetist, who will reply that when a patient no longer knows that "seven" comes after "six" then she is drugged and ready for operation.

It is of course easy to foresee a number of cases when a "normal" response would strike the informed as mad. For instance, you obviously presumed that I was engaged in the language game of counting, while in fact I could have been performing a naming ceremony. In that case, the proper response would not have been "seven" but "Gunnar," for what I had used were the abstract labels "1 . . . 6" to denote unknown members of my audience and the name "Gunnar" to denote myself. What an excellent illustration of the fact that "we cannot think what we cannot think; so what we cannot think we cannot *say* either."[11] The conclusion is that what the solipsist *"means* is quite correct; only it cannot be *said,* but makes itself manifest. The world is *my* world: this is manifest in the fact that the limits of *language* (of that language which alone I understand) mean the limits of *my* world."[12] But what does it mean to point? And what is the function of naming?

It is sometimes held that the proper name provides a key to knowledge; to know is to state what is identical to what. The name identifies. At the same time, however, naming a thing effectively drives a wedge between the namer and the named; naming *is* a queer connection

---

11.   *Tractatus,* 5.61.
12.   *Tractatus,* 5.62.

The Eye and the Index Finger

between a word and an object. Notwithstanding, the meaning of a name is sometimes explained by pointing to its bearer. "But that does not make the word ['this'] into a name. On the contrary: for a name is not used with, but only explained by means of, the gesture of pointing."[13] The fact remains, however, that the act of pointing is related to the ritual of baptizing. At the same time, it is clearly possible to think not only of what *is* the case but also of what is *not* the case.

It should now be clear that the possibility of cheating and deceiving is an integral part of language itself. It seems to follow that terms like "fair game," "causal prediction," and "blind obedience" have less to do with detached science and more to do with engaging morality. The reason is that an ostensive definition always can be interpreted in different ways. The lesson is that it is the possibility of various interpretations that at the same time is the threat and the driving force to truth. Such is the normative structure of the already-but-not-yet of the social and human sciences.

The social sciences and their languages are completely intertwined. Not only is human action thoroughly self-referential, but every utterance contains a crucial element of persuasion. There is no description without performance. Incredible truths are not truths at all, for truth is less an issue of what is the case and more an issue of credibility. To be a true scientist is consequently to be a performing artist, for to be an artist is to see a form in the invisible. But even though theory is the death of desire, desire is the birth of theory.

What is desire? Where is a symbol fertile enough to embody it and pregnant enough to bring it forth?

---

13.   *Philosophical Investigations,* 45.

An obvious candidate is the Saussurean concept of a sign, i.e.,

$$\text{sign} = \frac{\text{signifier}}{\text{signified}}$$

Of particular interest here is the limiting penumbra through which signifier and signified are kept together and apart. It is to this Bar of Categorical Meetings that I go to search for fractions of taboo-ridden phenomena and taboo-ridden insights. Intuition tells me that it is in the abyss of this power-filled void that visible becomes invisible, untouchable touchable. It is here that presence meets absence, absence meets presence. It is in the carnival at the bar that body is transubstantiated into meaning, meaning into body. Here I meet the other, full of dreams, full of realities. Thus, whereas Wittgenstein limits himself to the proposal that "where our language suggests a body and there is none: there we should like to say, is a *spirit*."[14] I would add that where we imagine a spirit, there is in reality a *body*. The totality, though, is in the intercourse of the two, one on top of the other, the other on top of the one. There are braids of desire like

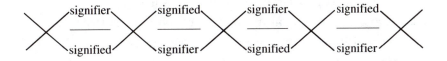

---

14.   *Philosophical Investigations*, 36.

Understanding these intertwined relations is to realize that every sign confounds not only the Cartesian categories of mind and matter but also the Lacanian categories of real and symbolic. Within itself, the sign contains those processes of ontological transformation that provide the liberating and repressive machinery of power. It is in the revel at the Saussurean Bar that "the speaking subject undergoes a transition to a void, to zero: loss of identity, afflux of drive and a return of symbolic capacities, but this time in order to take control of *drive* itself. This is precisely what expands the limits of the signifiable: a new aspect of the displacement between the referent/ signifiable, a new aspect of body, has thus found its signification."[15]

It is authors like Norbert Elias, Michel Foucault, Pierre Bourdieu, and Michel de Certeau who have illustrated how cultural conceptions of body and soul determine the boundaries between you and me. Mechanisms of signification indeed reflect and constitute the powerfilled techniques of disciplining, surveilling, ordering, and punishing. The insight inherited from Nietzsche is that I simultaneously *have* a body and *am* a body. As I live in and through language, so I live in and through my body; my body is neither thing nor idea but the measure of things. Like Maurice Merleau-Ponty, I thus conceive of the body as my mode of existence—through my body I express a knowledge that is not objective but existential. To form subjects is consequently to form bodies, especially to redraw the boundaries of the body. It is significant that whereas Michel Foucault devoted his life to studies of the constitution of the subject, Anthony Giddens entitled one of his books *The Constitution of Society.*

The physical limit of the body is marked by its own skin. Since boundaries tend to be guarded by the taboo, it is not surprising that the mode of touch is strictly regulated by rules of behavior. Thrusting into another person is clearly to transgress the boundaries of her self and this is regardless of whether the violation is through horrible rape or irresistible love.[16] It follows that to manipulate the body of others is to engage in a kind

---

15.   *The Speaking Subject,* pp. 217f.
16.   Here attention should be drawn to Hélène Cixous's remark that "bisexuality on an unconscious level is the possibility of extending into the other, of being in such a relation with the other that *I* move into the other without destroying the other: that I will look for the other where s/he is without trying to

of political anatomy. It also follows that experimenting with your own body is a sophisticated technique for learning who you are. My skin is escape-proof, the mode of understanding self-referential. Indeed, "if we were to make completely explicit the architectonics of the human body, its ontological framework, and how it sees itself and hears itself, we would see that the structure of its mute world is such that all the possibilities are already given in it."[17] Every text is a metaphor of the body, every mark a limiting sign of difference. Painters often claim that what they look at looks at them.

And thus it was that Paul Cézanne could make his revolutionary discoveries in visual art. Since he never took anything for granted, he could suddenly realize that he no longer painted landscapes but literally pictures, not mountains and houses but triangles and rectangles, not content but form. What he was losing was actually perspective, that single point of vision that hitherto had stabilized what people saw. In his acts of deconstruction, he rediscovered the art of hieroglyphic writing, where it is so clear that the cultural bounds of meaning are contained within the bodily limits of form. Nothing is without limits.

Given these relations between physical form and symbolic meaning, it is easy to appreciate why Jacques Derrida's conception of grammatology rests so securely in the two disciplines of geometry and psychoanalysis. While the former teach the techniques of making distinctions by drawing limiting lines, the latter warn that no line is to be trusted; the taken-for-granted is not in the content of the distinguished but rather in the marks of distinguishing. The thinner the boundary between you and me, the greater the risks and the stronger the taboos.[18] The stronger the taboos, the more

----

bring everything back to myself" (Hélène Cixous, *Castration or Decapitation,* p. 55).
17.   Maurice Merleau-Ponty, *The Visible and the Invisible,* p.155.
18.   In Dostoevsky's novel *The Double,* the low-ranking clerk Golyadkin hires a magnificient carriage to take him down the Nevsky Prospekt. He wishes to impress. But suddenly another carriage pulls up alongside his. Inside it sits not a woman to be seduced, but his superior Andrei Filipovich to be obeyed. No place to hide. Caught where he should not be. The other had come too close. Eventually Golyadkin was to go mad:

"Should I bow or shouldn't I? Should I acknowledge him? Admit that it is me? Or should I pretend I'm someone else, someone strikingly resembling me,

important to know. Conversely, keeping a distance is considered proper behavior, to be fostered and rewarded. Perhaps it is to Euclid and Freud that I should direct my questions of why it is so difficult to draw the lines differently. Nietzsche, Husserl, Heidegger, and Derrida come to mind as well. The conclusion is tempting: If the world is a synthesis of meaning, then the synthesis of meaning is itself the body. As Merleau-Ponty put it, "We have to reject the age-old assumptions that put the body in the world and the seer in the body, or, conversely, the world and the body in the seer as in a box. Where are we to put the limit between the body and the world, since the world is flesh?"[19]

The categorizing practices of pointing and naming indicate how shared knowledge is obtained through various forms of distanciation. Language is by nature a separation. As if to underscore its own point, this performing essay is itself an instance of the same practices of removal. The only senses I have relied on are those of sight and hearing (assuming, of course, that you have been sensitive enough to read aloud). Your eyes and ears have picked up signals from my voice and hand, especially from my index finger elongated into a real pen and into an imagined pointer. There is no coincidence that the eye and the pointer are the masculine organs of Newtonian physics, that physics which—like geography—deals with action at a distance. All disciplines have their gravity models, don't they?

---

and look completely indifferent?'' Golyadkin asked himself in indescribable anguish.

''Yes, that's it: I'm not me and that's all there is to it.'' So he thought, his eyes fixed on Andrei Filipovich as he took off his hat to him.

''I, I, I . . . no, nothing, sir,'' he stammered in a whisper. ''The fact is, it's not me. . . . Yes, that's all there is to it.''

Quoted in Marshal Berman, *All That Is Solid Melts into Air*, p. 211.

19.   *The Visible and the Invisible*, p. 138.

Einsteinian physics, on the other hand, deals with action by contact; since the mutual action of two electrically charged bodies depends on the character of the intervening medium, the message written by the two bodies depends on the context within which it is written. Kissing a Russian on the mouth is not the same as licking the ass of a Swede. Moskovskaya is not Absolut.

What now, if I had produced a text that did not involve my hand and your eyes, but rather my tongue and your nose. Is it even possible to imagine a written document where I did not sit in my study distancing myself not only from you, the reader, but indeed from the very paper onto which I project my marks? Imagine if this text suddenly came really close, sniffing, farting, dripping! You should then say something like "I have gone mad." Difficult even in the deceitful theater. Impossible in a truthful publication. Plato again!

Flight of fancy! May be. The unthinkable thought experiment is nevertheless illustrative, for it clearly reveals the role of limits in social discourse. Yet there are of course things one can do in the theater that are impossible in the university. Yet it is generally held that creative change always occurs at the boundaries, never at the center. The trick is to mix genres, for it is the nonclassifiable that initiates new processes. But only processes smell.

One who successfully approached these limits was Georges Bataille, not the least in his pornographic novel *The Story of the Eye*. On reading this work, it is crucial to realize that its main characters are not the two individuals of Simone and Marcelle. The lead actors are rather a cast of metaphors, especially that of the eye. In its search of meaning, this strange creature wanders from the socket of the face to the suck-it of the cunt. Tsch, tsch! What pushes this imaginary into new symbolic forms is indeed the physical form itself; the spheric eye is metamorphosed first into an egg and then into a testicle. And then suddenly, "there in the sunlight, on Simone's seat, lay a white dish containing two balls, glands the size and shape of eggs, and of a pearly whiteness, faintly bloodshot like the globe of an eye."[20]

---

20. Georges Bataille, *The Story of the Eye,* p. 51. The original reads: "à la

Immediately after the bullfight, under the sun of Seville, the narrator fuses together the killing of the bull, the loss of the toreador's eye, and Simone's orgasm on the plate of testicles: "Thus, two globes of equal size and consistency had suddenly been propelled in opposite directions at once. One, the white ball of the bull, had been thrust into the 'pink and dark' cunt that Simone had bared in the crowd; the other, a human eye, had spurted from Grenaro's head with the same force as a bundle of innards from a belly. This coincidence, tied to death through a sort of urinary liquefaction of the sky, first brought us back to Marcelle in a moment that was so brief and almost substantial, yet so uneasily vivid that I stepped forward like a sleepwalker as though about to touch *her* at eye level."[21]

It is obvious from these quotations that Bataille's story is less about perverse sexuality and more about the techniques of creativity. A similar but less revolting example of a metaphor on the loose is Gogol's classical story of the nose. Here the human form is broken into surreal fragments as the barber Ivan Jakovlevich recognizes that the nose he discovers in his morning loaf of bread actually belongs to one of his customers. Will he throw it in the Neva or give it back to its rightful owner? An ad in the paper solves the problem. By treating the unreal as real, Gogol here illustrated how humor can serve as a means of insight and change.

As Jacques Derrida has remarked, understanding the relation between metaphor and creativity is "to undertake a general reversal of metaphorical directions."[22] We must allow ourselves to be carried away, not only forward but backward as well. Literally. Hence bodily. Yet, whenever a metaphor is let on the loose, the reader easily loses his way. Old

---

place où mon amie devait s'asseoir reposaient sur une assiette les deux couilles nues; ces glandes, de la grosseur et de la forme d'un oeuf, étaient d'une blancheur nacrée, rosie de sang, analogue à celle du globe oculaire" (*Histoire de l'oeil*, p. 76).
21. *The Story of the Eye*, p. 54. In the original (p. 81): "Deux globes de même grandeur et consistance s'étaient animés de mouvements contraires et simultanés. Un testicule blanc de taureau avait pénétré la chair 'rose et noire' de Simone: un oeil était sorti de la tête de jeune homme. Cette coïncidence liée en même temps qu'à la mort à une sorte de liquéfaction urinaire du ciel, un moment, me rendit Marcelle. Il me sembla, dans cet insaisissable instant, la toucher."
22. Jacques Derrida, *Dissemination,* p. 81.

lighthouses begin to blink in strange patterns. No longer can I figure out my position. There is nevertheless consolation in Wittgenstein's aphorism that "a philosophical problem has the form: I don't know my way about."[23] For an old-time geographer, it is interesting to note that space tends to be associated with corporeality.

And thus it is that the tremulous body is a means of meaning. The eye and the index finger become metaphors for grasping the distanciation inherent in all subject formation. Our only contact with the world is through the holes of our bodies. It is through them that individuals are penetrated by society and its accepted norms of thought-and-action. It is by such bodily means that you and I become obedient and predictable. But it is also through these same organs that you and I penetrate others and thereby the world. It is through them that we breathe and survive but also suffocate and decay.

Now it seems plausible: the concept of trust has its social origin and destination in the unconscious of the body. But to be trustworthy is nothing less than to be predictable. The screws tighten. "Fucking you" has a double ring. The symbol of marriage is likewise. The double doubles up.

Once again, the suspicion is this: our words get their meaningful power less from the things they refer to and more from the taken-for-granted of their physicality. As Roland Barthes put it: "Language is a skin . . . I rub against the other. It is as if I had words instead of fingers, or fingers at the tip of my words. My language trembles with desire. . . . Language experiences orgasm upon touching itself."[24]

Whenever I rub my skin against the other, I experiment with the limits

23. *Philosophical Investigations,* 123.
24. Roland Barthes, *A Lover's Discourse,* p. 73.

of the subject. But the skin of a word delimits its cultural meaning. Whenever I let my words touch the words of another, then, by necessity, I bring forth new meanings and new takens-for-granted. Yet, it should be recalled that even though desire is the birth of theory, theory is the death of desire. The reason is that to create is not to have an idea that searches for its expression, but to have an expression that searches for its meaning.

So: Hold the expressions in the palm of your hand. Mold them there only to let them move on to the tender tips of your fingers. And they will come. Soft and clean. For it is exactly in the crevice between presence and absence that language becomes erotic. The secret is not in the conventional metaphors of desire but in the devious desires of metaphor. Yet, the telos is less in semantics and more in syntax, less in what I am talking about and more in the way I order about what I am talking about. It is syntax that leads me by the hand; "I really do think with my pen, because my head often knows nothing about what my hand is writing."[25]

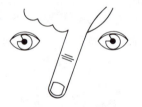

Through this performing essay, I have entered a zone beyond the frontier lines of a humanistic social science. Once there I have tried to decode those sign systems which make you and me so obedient and so predictable. I have hoped to show what cannot be said and to say what cannot be shown: a juggling of fragments, an intertextual search for a body beyond the alphabet. To communicate is to participate in that which is manifest.

What I have illustrated is the obvious: even in phallologocentric writing desire streams through some kind of body. In its rhythmic movements, texts are like kites: at a distance they are like free birds set against the sky; in reality, though, they are tied down with the strings of social convention.

---

25. Ludwig Wittgenstein, *Culture and Value*, p. 17.

What is this word "word"? How do I use my fingers to touch its limits and thereby those everyday practices that simultaneously keep individual and society together and apart? How do I sense not the eye but the seeing of the eye? How do I discover the alphabet of the body in the body of the alphabet?

More questions than answers. And thus it is appropriate to close with a quote from Merleau-Ponty, who quotes Váléry, who quotes someone else, who quotes God knows who: "Language is everything, since it is the voice of no one, since it is the voice of the things, the waves, and the forests. And what we have to understand is that there is no dialectical reversal from one of these views to the other; we do not have to reassemble them into a synthesis: they are two aspects of the reversibility which is the ultimate truth."[26]

---

26.   *The Visible and the Invisible,* p. 155. "Och i en mening är språket allt, som Valéry säger, eftersom det inte är någons röst, utan själva tingens, vågornas och skogarnas röst. Och vad det gäller att förstå är att det mellan dessa båda åskådningar inte föreligger någon dialektisk omkastning, vi behöver inte sammanföra dem till en syntes: de är två aspekter av den omvändbarhet som är slutlig sanning." Translated in *Kris,* p. 75.

Hooked

"You say I and you are proud of this little word. But greater than your word is your body which does not say I but performs I." Thus spoke Nietzsche in his Zarathustra.

Nietzsche's insight was that the identity of an individual is intimately tied to the fact that he simultaneously *has* a body and *is* a body. I am limited by my own skin and this is why physical touch tends to be taboo. To penetrate another person is to transgress the boundaries of her self, to trespass and to sin. To experiment with one's own body is therefore a sophisticated technique for investigating who you are. Your skin is escape-proof.

Investigating the prison of the body naturally leads to questions that no culture can afford. The collective forms a common front against the explorers at the outer limits of existence. It is at this limiting line that moral indignation is concentrated into points of physical violence, nowadays often disguised as legal obligation. Uniformed guards prove with their own bodies how correct Nietzsche really was.

• • •

One to take Nietzsche's insight seriously is the remarkable body artist Mr. Stelarc. During the summer of 1985 he exhibited, lectured, and performed at the Fools Festival in Copenhagen. As expected, his presence stirred much attention. As a consequence, he was also prohibited from carrying out his most spectacular plan. His hope had been to rise into the evening sky dangling under a balloon, hung in eighteen ropes that, by means of a kind of fish hook, had been pierced through the skin of his back, arms, and legs. But when the balloonist understood what Stelarc had in mind, there arose a number of practical and financial problems. In the end, the role of the balloon was taken over by a huge construction crane.

•

Stelarc was born in 1946 on the island of Cyprus. As a young boy he moved with his parents to Melbourne, Australia. Since 1970 he has lived in Japan, teaching art and sociology at the Yokohama International School. From the beginning he was called "Stelios Arcadiou," but for simplicity's sake he himself merged this denotation into "Stelarc." This is now the only name that appears in his Australian passport: an intentional forgery of origin, another experiment with identity.

When not engaged in his path-breaking artistic work, Stelarc lives a conventional life with his Mexican-born wife, Judith, and their two daughters, Astra and Nova. He pays his body sufficient respect to abstain from tobacco, alcohol, and other drugs. He is built like a statue, balding with Mediterranean hair around his neck, on his chest and his shoulders. His hands are openly expressive, his eyes soft yet intensive. As if they had seen something beautiful, impossible to forget. The accent is Australian, the laughter bubbling yet slightly forced, solitary rather than infectious. In all his professionalism he is full of humor. Is he beginning to catch a glimpse of himself? Is this why he projects a sense of peace and trust?

●

Stelarc's explorations are philosophically and artistically well founded, permeated by a vision of biological evolution. His main thesis is that the human body has reached a stage at which it has ceased to develop on its own. This to him explains why we have been invaded by miniature technology like wristwatches, contact lenses, false teeth, and artificial hearts. These are tendencies Stelarc welcomes. He calls himself a bionaut.

In the beginning, Stelarc performed his explorations by means of small video cameras. Peeping through one's own asshole certainly offers an unusual perspective on the world; realizing that we suddenly watch the watching we cannot hold our laughter.

In the same spirit, Stelarc has undertaken a number of experiments with his own body sounds. In the sculpturing studio at the Danish Art Academy, he demonstrated aspects of this work. By controlling his muscles in a yogalike fashion, he staged a peculiar kind of concert in which his eyelids, heart, abdomen, and blood turned into instruments with characteristic tones. These were monitored through microphones fastened to his skin, transmitted through a jumble of circuits to a synthesizer where they were mixed and finally thrown out through a number of loudspeakers. Horrible whining when he wrinkled his forehead, but the rhythm of his blood was like the surge of the sea. And there he stood in his nakedness, his inner life projected onto a screen of fluorescent light. His artificial third hand opened and closed. It could write as well.

The most intensive experience came toward the end of the thirty-minute happening. Via small mirrors fastened to his eyelids he projected two laser beams onto a screen at the opposite end of the room. The patterns he drew were completely beautiful. Suddenly it was obvious that here was an individual who had liberated himself from his body through his body. The artist and his work had merged into one. From the conception of the body as metaphor had sprung an identity of a higher order. The brilliant dance of the laser cats contained traces of a choreography of meaning.

And the next evening the show went on. This time Stelarc devoted his attention to gravity itself, for he is obsessed with the dream of floating freely, with the idea of experiencing his body as its own support. Outside the Royal Theater thousands had gathered to witness how he was to hang himself above the city roofs, dangling in his own meat. Many had come for the same reasons that at other times take them to the football field and the boxing ring. For "it surely hurts," says Stelarc. "But a masochist I ain't. Also women give birth in pain."

The event is carefully planned. Chosen helpers insert the stainless hooks into anatomically secure positions. Kurt Larsen—the crane operator—climbs to his position dressed in the yellow T-shirt of his company. How horribly high it is. The long arm of the crane makes a trial swing above the city block. The wire is lowered, Stelarc hooked.

And slowly he is lifted to the sky, arms outstretched as into a blessing, head high. The body swings. The wind chills. The spectators wonder whether he feels pain or whether he will fall down, torn from himself by himself. But nobody knows that he suffers from vertigo.

After twenty minutes he is cautiously lowered to the ground, landing on a mattress. Cut loose, clean wounds. A cup of sweet tea, a blanket, some calming words. Suddenly he stands up again, walking on bare feet into a camper to get dressed. The door is closed. All is over.

Crucified, elevated, again descended. This time in Denmark. Next in Brazil. Earlier in Australia, Japan, Mexico, and the United States. Twenty-three times suspended. Which double functions does he serve, Mr. Stelarc?

•

Fifteen hours later we meet again to sooth his wounds with philosophic talk. Fully alive. All together. Brimming with impressions. "Copenhagen was so incredibly beautiful. Not a sound to be heard. Only the roaring wind and the small vibrations in my own skin. In borderland I was. Like a wind tunnel. How long can anyone remain there and get away with it?"

So he wonders, the artist who tries to understand who he is. In the meantime I cannot free myself from the memory of those eternal minutes during which he had been floating above the heads of the city's intoxicated youth. Once again like one of Chagall's blue brides, over a landscape full of mythical symbols. Little did the crowd understand the artist's courage, for how many have read their Nietzsche or even their Canetti? What some nevertheless seemed to catch was a glimpse of the beauty in the celestial body suspended in the no-man's-land of the lawless. But in Japan, the same body is taken to court, charged with pornographic activity. The reason is that he performs his suspension with his pubic hair unshaven. The unusual takes unusual forms.

●　　●　　●

Thus he appears in his incredible force, the explorer of the limits of the self. The remarkable is that others are shocked. But once more the social forces show themselves to be as implacable as the physical. Both serve the same double function: of keeping the deviant in place.

Nothing unusual about that. But he who questions his body, thereby questions his culture.

Hemming the Way

The subject of this essay is La Contessa. Its guiding image is the self-referential circle, that most natural and most totalizing of all forms. And yet it should be noted that even though the circle often is interpreted as a symbol of renewal, it also encapsulates the absence of time and space.

Since the circle has neither beginning nor end, neither up nor down, it carries within itself a hint of a world without categories, perhaps even of a geography without time or space. This is an extremely challenging conception, for it is only by trying to imagine a geography without spatial relations that we can begin to appreciate the limiting nature of our discipline. As Hegel used to teach, we can fully grasp a given thought position only by understanding both what it can and what it cannot do. Tell me who you are not, and through that denial I shall tell you who you are. The road to the I goes via the Other.

The symbol of the circle is closely related to the symbol of the wheel. At the center of the wheel there is always a nave. And since the theory and practice of geography is an intellectual endeavor, I now baptize this nave with the name "meaning." I choose this term, for I believe it is toward the concept of meaning that all studies are aiming. But just as I am intrigued by the image of a placeless geography, so I am intrigued by the idea of a meaningless statement. And for the same reasons. For even though the idea of a meaningless statement may be impossible, it is certainly not meaningless. The thought of the meaningless is itself meaningful, for it is only through the meaningless that the meaningful can be delimited.

•

The concept of meaning comes close to the Saussurean concept of signified. But just as there can be no meaning without a meaning-bearer, so there can be no signified without a signifier. Every sign is indeed such that everything interesting happens in that thin penumbra that simultaneously keeps signifier and signified together and apart. It is in the transcendence of the bar that the physicality of the signifier is penetrated by cultural meanings and the untouchable of the signified is embraced by sensible expressions. But most expressions have more than one meaning, just as most meanings have more than one expression. It follows that even though meaning might be produced as an effect, the meaning of a sign is never totally predictable. Like the I itself, it is always unfinished.

Since meaning is a cultural construct, it is thoroughly context-dependent. New meanings consequently emerge from the interface between one context and another. And thus it is that a change in meaning means a change in central beliefs. One taken-for-granted touches another and there is a moment of erotic fulfillment. But at the same time there is a moment of madness.

Does this mean that to be mad is to approach the meaningless? Perhaps. Because in such situations I am utterly on my own, I am not like anybody else, I have no rules to follow, no fixes to keep me steady. Viewed in this perspective, meaning shows itself as what it really is: an instrument of socialization, a standardized tool designed to make you and me norm(al) and alike. Just as there can be no private language, there can be no private meaning. The so-called meaningless is a private silence, the so called meaningful a public chatter.

One meaning of meaning is obviously to make you and me obedient and predictable. Like the language in which it is expressed, meaning enters as an ingredient in the ethical glue that fastens individual to society and society to individual. Perhaps it takes a madman or a solipsist to illustrate what a meaningful geography actually could be. The only trouble is that the normal reader would never know, for that which falls outside the taken-for-granted always goes unnoticed. The paradox is, though, that so does that which falls inside the taken-for-granted. The secret is in the word itself: the taken-for-granted is everything we think-and-do without thinking-and-doing. It follows that language by necessity is self-referential. But so is geography. For a geography without language is as unthinkable as a language without meaning. Meaning is indeed a perfect example of the infolding of language; meaning is self-reference par excellence.

• • •

Implicit in these opening paragraphs is the idea of the geographer as a loving artist, not as an obedient apparatchik. The artist has no choice but always to stand inside himself and outside of society. But why should he aim for the impossible? Why should he try to express the meaningless?

The answer is that it is only from the position within himself that he can say anything different and therefore worthwhile—a language understandable to others can never communicate the profoundly personal, for to communicate is to repeat the conventions of that which we share in common. But this you know already and for two opposite reasons. First, because you experience yourself as a unique human being; you are you and they are they and the twain shall never meet. Second, because you have been taught the dogma of objectivity and scientific methodology; the so-called truth must be able to be verified by anyone else. My own personal insights are of no interest, for in science it is my duty to make myself dumber than I am. In order to communicate and accumulate knowledge, I must look at the world not directly with my own eyes but through the normalizing spectacles of the scientific community. In principle, then, the scientist is as replaceable and exchangeable as any other capitalist worker. The artist is different, at least if she is not a social realist and hence a politician and not an artist at all. As Nietzsche had it, the idea is to transform oneself into a work of art.

Toward this background, it becomes clear that the foundation of geography and other social sciences is not in empirical observations of the conventional kind. The primary data are in fact not in the landscapes I can see and touch, but in the written or spoken sentences I can read or hear. The proper place of geography is in the books, or rather in the interpretation or meaningful translations of various texts. You cannot have a dissertation without words, you know. Neither can you have a string of words without meaning.

The old insight returns again: meaning is like understanding; never direct, always indirect; never time and place invariant, always context-dependent. Geography is indeed what geographers do and that explains why even a solidified discipline can change. Whether we like it or not, geography is an intellectual enterprise, regardless of whether it is conducted in the field or in the library. Possessing a pen and a language is nevertheless more indispensable than donning a pair of boots and a measuring rod.

And yet. A scientific geographer who actively pursues the concept of meaning is a rare bird. The concepts of truth and lawlike statements are a little easier, even though they happen to be closely related to meaning itself. For this reason I now intend to illuminate the concept of meaning through some quick reflections from the theory of truth.

● ● ●

The first spotlight I switch on was manufactured by members of the old Vienna circle. As recalled, they argued that a meaningful statement must meet the double requirement of being logically consistent and empirically true. Put differently, the meaningful must be doubly anchored in well defined principles of thought on the one hand and in common observations of facts on the other.

On the surface, the two requirements may appear quite different. In reality, however, they are permeated by the same ideal of perfect communication; we trust the principles of logic because we have been taught the same multiplication table and we trust physical observations because our own eyes tell us that this table is this table in this room and not an angel in heaven. These conditions of trust are indispensable, for without them it is impossible to agree that we are talking about the same things. And on that assumption rests first the ideal of perfect communication and then the possibility of accumulating knowledge; just as the fundamental driving force of capitalism is to accumulate capital, so the overriding concern of science is to accumulate knowledge. Stone upon stone, thesis upon thesis. But the task of accumulating knowledge puts highly specific demands on the syntax and semantics of the language within which the accumulation occurs. In particular, this ideal dialect must surrender to the forces of certainty and stability. Its worst enemy is ambiguity, regardless of whether the ambiguous is in the thoughts or in the observations. Precision is achieved through stabilization of the language I am thinking *in* and of the phenomena I am speaking *about.*

And yet. Even logical empiricism is submerged in a hermeneutics of suspicion. A statement anchored only in thought or only in observations is obviously not as trustworthy as one that is anchored in both at the same time. My thoughts can be badly thought, just as my vision can be badly distorted. The credibility of my propositions clearly increases if I can state the same message both in the language of logics and in the language of observations. Every law is a law of the double.

The positivist is of course highly particular about what he considers admissible reasoning and admissible observations. It is in these particularities—and only there—that the alternative theories differ. For instance, the Marxist replaces conventional logic with dialectics, but he retains much of the positivist's view of what counts as an empirical fact. In contrast, the surrealist tends not only to reason dialectically, but also to include within reality that which lies over the roofs and beyond the senses; for him the real ceases to be corporeal and becomes superreal. To be a true individual—i.e., a true artist—is to him to be different from the rest. It is his highest ambition to communicate this unique and noncommunicable. Yet he realizes, of course, that reaching this goal is impossible.

Different as they may be, the positivist, the Marxist, and the surrealist all share the view that to be meaningful a statement must be doubly anchored—in here and out there. Where they differ is mainly in their attitudes toward communication, social control, and private freedom. Oversimplified, the positivist tends to focus on the physicality of the signifier and the surrealist on the meanings of the signified. Both are realists, but they differ in how they delimit reality. It is crucial to acknowledge, however, that their different emphases reflect different attitudes to the crisis of the sign.

This crisis became acute with Mallarmé and it has been a major driving force in all intellectual developments thereafter. To me, the postmodernism of the last twenty-five years is merely the awareness of this crisis brought to a higher level. The crisis consists in a heightened awareness of the fact that word and object are not the same; when I say the word "table" that does not make me into a table. Indeed, there are no words for that which I value most. What is meaningful to me as a unique human being becomes destroyed and meaningless as soon as I try to catch it in the language net of common sense. All I can do is to repeat common lies and common conventions. And that is why the autistic child preserves its integrity by refusing to speak. Only a shade of blue is precise enough. In communicating, we detect the babble of the collective and the silence of the individual; there is a common in common sense and a solitude in the lonesome crowd. We are deafened by the cries of the former and responding to the whispers of the latter. There is indeed a social space of silence, for with Kant space became a form of understanding.

●　　●　　●

An echo. Is it not echoes that we are condemned to produce and reproduce? Traces of copies, copies of traces. And here is another instance where it becomes clear that also the geographer—simply because he is a living human—must be a kind of artist. As with anybody else, one of his major tasks is to produce a copy that is as true to his conception of the original as he can possibly make it. But even though the artist knows that he can never reach a perfect reproduction, he must never give up the attempt. The ideal can never be realized, for every meaning is contextual and every context is itself contextual. As soon as the interpreter begins his interpretation, he becomes a part of the interpreted.

The deed and the doer can in deed not be separated. Every interpretation is embedded in a form of life; that is why interpretations are so crucially important. It is for their sake that people kill and get killed. And this is regardless of the particular truth theory through which life and world are made to hang together. It is dogmatism that falsifies and perspecitivism that brings coherence and thereby meaning into fragments.

Perspectivism is a metabelief that contrasts with both dogmatism and nihilism. With its divergent styles of research, presentations, and representations, it characterizes the discipline of geography. To exemplify, I shall now draw attention to three highly different interpretations of cities. In the process, I hope to throw additional light on the concept of meaning and its relations to the mentioned theories of truth.

●

My first example comes from the mathematical geography that many were engaged in twenty years ago and that some are continuing still. Central to this perspective was the image of a socioeconomic landscape of hills and valleys, where the peaks represent the centers of activity and the depressions the outlying areas of little concern. This abstract landscape is of course a heritage from classical location theory, but it is beautifully depicted in the computer maps of a Waldo Tobler and in the equations of a Leslie Curry and a Yorgo Papageorgiou.

The driving force behind these equations is a wish to produce a copy of reality as abstract and as general as any mind can imagine. The search is for *the* proper expression, i.e., for that specific signifier or formula which somehow matches the assumptions and worldviews inherent in the theory, i.e., in the signified. As always, the total signs get their meaning from the employed inference rules. The latter tend to come from probability theory and they somehow invoke the power of a mystical force playing a game of solitaire with loaded dice. The wave-like surface expands and detracts by sucking on its own nipples. And here I am reminded not of the stochastic urn models but instead of Mallarmé, who wrote in his *Coup de dés* that "nothing will have taken place except the place. Except perhaps a constellation"—a constellation of the determined rules of the game and the haphazardous playing of the game.

It is as an abstract and beautiful copy of this original conception of the world that I interpret the equations of quantitative geography when it is at its best. From another perspective, these meaningful attempts of rerendering the world may themselves appear meaningless. As an example, Willy Kyrklund, the exclusive Swedish writer, once wondered like this: "Must we not call the game of dice a difficult game, a very difficult game? For who can say about himself: 'I have achieved perfect mastery of the game of dice'? Even if you practice, even if you attain a considerable experience in the game of dice, you will never reach a mastery worthy of the name. But the rules are simple, very simple. The stones rattle along the mountain side, rolling and rolling."

But through the rattling of the murmuring stones that roll down the gravity slope of the demand cone, I can still hear the surge of the Fourier waves as they hit the shores of Traditional Geography: hhhhh hhhhh hhhhh. If this is not an illustration of the art of geography, then I do not know what it is. A garden of Jean Arp sculptures.

●

A different constellation of significr and signified is in my second example. This comes from the Marxist geography that I associate mainly with David Harvey. As the restless analyst I know him to be, he manages to merge within the individual of his own body and mind, his total experiences of literature, social science, thought and action. In the tradition of dialectics, his writing practices the mediating processes of reflection and speculation, where everything hangs together with everything else; the art is to see a world in a grain of sand. The theory of truth is therefore not one of piecemeal correspondence but instead one of totalizing coherence. Dialectics is in fact to be understood as a mode of life, not as a technique of scientific management; a statement made in the language of dialectics is validated less through deliberate reasoning and more through reflective action.

While the mathematical geographers work primarily on the nominator or signifier part of the sign, a Marxist like Harvey tends to pay more attention to the denominator or the signified part. It is of course true that his starting point usually is in the physical landscape of roads, houses, factories, schools, shops and so on, but having sipped inspiration from these initial objectifications, he quickly slides under the Saussurean Bar. Once there he runs into the category of social class and the two get into a bacchanalian revel of how the contradictions of capitalist logic can be interpreted and eventually reconciled in an *aufgehoben* state. But also in that conversation, it is the rules of inference that give the signs their meaning.

In the case of the Marxists, these inferences are geared less toward understanding the world and more toward changing it. And yet they paradoxically acknowledge that the new must somehow grow out of the old. There is an image of an already-but-not-yet, of an oak in an acorn and a man in a boy. This quickly raises the issue of whether the Marxist version of the world presents a good copy or merely a passable forgery. The distinction is that a good copy expresses both the precise surface features and the ambiguous meanings inherent in the original. A copy that deconstructs itself along the same path as the original is indeed a rare constellation, perhaps an instance of restless analysis.

•

The restless remembrance of things past is itself written into the crisis of the sign. Rarely has this been better demonstrated than in the surrealist literature about the city.

The objective of the surrealist movement was to achieve an infinite expansion of reality. Like the Marxists, the surrealists wanted to transform the world. But the latter saw clearly that this required them to deconstruct the sign itself, to assault the very language through which the world hangs together. More specifically, they realized first that the tangible of the signifier conceals the marvelous of the signified, and then that this marvelous can be revealed by diverting words and objects from their familiar contexts. The reader or viewer should be jolted into novel chains of association through deliberate changes of context. The strategy is of course to play with the insight that just as meaning is context-dependent, so is context meaning-dependent. As Louis Aragon put it, "The idea of limit is the only inconceivable idea; . . . logic is merely a means of raising us to the level of metaphysics: and it should not forget that fact."

It is obvious that the issues of representation were as crucial to the surrealists as to anybody else. In André Breton's own words: "Reciprocal love, such as I envisage it, is a system of mirrors which reflects for me, under the thousand angles that the unknown can take for me, the faithful image of the one I love, always more surprising in her divining of my own desire and more gilded with life." The point at stake, however, is not mimicry but creation. While most scientists and conventional artists try to achieve some sort of equivalence between copy and original, both the surrealists and the postmodernists try to subtract one set of associations from the other; the greater the disparity, the more powerful the light. To be an authentic actor of this type is to associate what is normally dissociated, and to dissociate what is normally associated. There is nevertheless a deep sense of humor in the craziness. How happy I would be if the reader of this text felt just a little like Benjamin Péret at the end of the world: Stupid like sausages whose sauerkraut has already been eaten away.

It is of course in a work like *Nadja* that the marvelous reality of the city is brought out most vividly. Despite the photographs, which serve as recollecting signifiers for the narrator, it is difficult to know whether the girl exists at all, for she is not as much a person as a state of mind; her way of thought governs her way of life. The same holds for Aragon's Paris Peasant, who in his dreams wonders: "How did the idea come about that it is the concrete which is the real? Is not the concrete, on the contrary, all that is beyond the real, is not the real the abstract judgement which the concrete presupposes only in the dialectical process? And does not the image, as such, possess its own reality which is its application to knowledge, its substitution for it? . . . Basically, no way of thought exists that is not an image. . . . Fact exists only in terms of time, that is to say of language."

• • •

And now I could go on communicating the noncommunicable. But even though the symbol of the circle has neither beginning nor end, an essay must sometimes take a break. Soon. What I have noted is how the self-referential question of language and representation quickly turns into the question of meaning. I then observed how the theories of meaning tie in with the theories of truth. But the alternative theories themselves reflect different attitudes to the modernist crisis of the sign. As a consequence, I closed with examples of how this crisis of representation has been approached within the discipline of geography. My particular illustrations were chosen on aesthetic rather than scientific grounds, for truth is not discovered but invented. Logic is itself permeated by rhetoric, the idea of truth by the notion of trust.

The overriding conclusion is that both meaning and truth are thoroughly contextual. Hence they are also thoroughly social. And so it is that the meaningless becomes so incredibly interesting, for it may be through the meaningless that the social reveals its true and profoundly repressive nature.

While I have concentrated on the relations between theories of meaning and theories of truth, I have left the relations between language, meaning, and intention virtually untouched. There may be another time and another place. But then it is possible that I will forget about it all, for intentions might be too important to write about. As Italo Calvino let Marco Polo say to Kublai Khan in their conversations about invisible cities, "Memory's images, once they are fixed in words, are erased. Perhaps I am afraid of losing Venice all at once, if I speak of it. Or perhaps, speaking of other cities, I have already lost it, little by little." Anybody familiar with Ernest Hemingway will know my destination: Across the river and into the mind.

PLANES

Lines of Power

For Jacques Lacan the unconscious was structured like a language. For me power is structured like a knowledge.

As I now move from this double beginning, I quickly find myself in the company of René Girard and his theory of mimetic desire. I am driven there by my conviction that knowledge by definition is an exercise in translation. But just as desire desires not to be satisfied, so a translation can never be perfect. And in this light, communication shows itself to be what it really is: a form of collective violence designed to neutralize the deviant by sacrificing it on the altar of social cohesion. The unknown must submit to the known just as the world is divided into reasonable and unreasonable. Subjects are produced through subjection, objects through objection.

Boiled down to its essentials, telling the truth is to claim that something is something else and be believed when you do it. Others trust me, when I say that this is thus or that a = b. To succeed in this tricky business is not so easy, however, for after Nietzsche everybody knows that this is this, not thus, that a equals a, not b. The similar and the same are similar, not same; there is never presence, only proximity. And with this reminder, I have already demonstrated how perfect knowledge is as impossible as perfect translation, how truth has more to do with trust and conviction than with what here-and-now happens to be the case. In addition, I have suggested that even though a and b are striving to become doubles of one another, this desire can never be fulfilled. Both knowledge and language require a defect or a fault, an alter ego who keeps his distance. The dynamics of power are rooted in difference.

●   ●   ●

What remains is a play of make-believe. To this end, I shall attempt a deconstruction of the word IS—the epistemological marker par excellence. Nobody can do without this sign of mimetic desire in concentration, for without it there would be neither understanding nor communication. Without IS nothing would be, not even Nothing.

At the same time, IS would not be IS if it did not have many meanings. It is indeed this ambiguity that turns the IS into a key concept in the vocabulary of power. Its nature is to be supplementary and constantly shifting; if captured in one context, it promptly escapes to another. As it performs its juggling tricks at Polity Fair, power stays in power because of its evasive anonymity; by manifesting itself it conceals itself; in hiding it shows. The word is the manifest nonexistence of what it designates.

To keep track of myself, I shall concretize some various meanings of the IS by constructing a set of straight lines. It is in the turning and twisting of these objective correlates that I shall then catch a glimpse of power with its pants down. A blue eye meets a brown, analyzing and experiencing in the same glance; the law itself as an instance of Epimenides' paradox of the right to say I: all Cretans are liars, for power is in that minuscule yet insurmountable space between speech and silence.

My first drawing of the IS consisted of two parallel lines, an equal sign of the type

$$=$$

During the first half of the 1970s, I spent some of my best years in the company of this symbol. Every evening we went to bed, every morning we had breakfast, every day we conversed. Bewitched, bothered, and bewildered. And yet. The emptiness between the two lines eventually melted away, the two became one, turned on the side, transcended itself, and became the slash of

$$/$$

In the mid-eighties, the potent angle changed once more as the line found a resting place in the Saussurean Bar of

$$\underline{\qquad}$$

While " $=$ " demarcates what is identical to what and "/" stands for the penumbra of a mutual relation, the "————" is the rendezvous of signifier and signified. While " $=$ " has its roots in logics and "/" comes from dialectics, "————" is central to semiotics. Regardless of these differences, however, the three signs are all possessed by the same kind of mimetic desire; what stands on one side of the line wants to merge with what stands on the other. But, here as elsewhere, the desire is defined by its impossibility.

The story of the straight line contains everything I know and everything I have not yet understood. This includes fragments of power. To me it is in the richness of these symbols—signs for the simultaneous splitting apart and joining together—that power reveals itself in its most clear, most elementary, most beautiful form. In comparison, the king's scepter, the general's baton, and the bishop's crosier appear as vulgar as the Danish emperor in his nakedness. It was Georges Bataille (*Visions of*

Excess, p. 5) who noted that "the *copula* of terms is no less irritating than the *copulation* of bodies."

• • •

If the equation is the wheel of positive science, then the equal sign is the nave of that wheel. The statements on each side of the sign should represent the same quantity, express the same amount, or say the same thing in different words. Clear enough. Yet there is a serious problem: since every reformulation by necessity is supplementary and therefore strictly speaking a distortion, a given supplement can sometimes be accepted as a truth, sometimes rejected as a lie. The issue is further complicated by the requirement that the reformulation should not only be true but also informative; whereas a tautology by definition is true but not informative, a metaphor is often informative but never true. Once again, it is not sufficient to note that something is the case. I must also be believed when I point it out: truth is not a private conviction, but a social convention. Truth is not truth unless shared. Hence, the statement $a = b$ becomes credible when it refers to phenomena that are open to common inspection, a condition that legitimizes the power of logical empiricism and grounds the metaphysics of presence. It is nevertheless an argument of postmodern deconstruction that such abilities to share the world must not be taken for granted. The pronouns I and he are radically different. It is not surprising that truth often is invoked as an excuse: "Objectively, Comrade!" — "Unconsciously, Sister!"

Indeed it now seems clear that every truth contains an element of distortion, of lying, of them overruling me. Every truth is inevitably formulated around a nucleus of difference, for knowing what something *is* involves knowing what it is *not.* In the public congregation of categorization new truths are being blessed and old prejudices sacrificed. Ecstasy is that brief moment of conversion in which one set of taken-for-granted is replaced by another. But what is it to change one's taken-for-granted?

To change one's taken-for-granted is to change one's central beliefs. It is in the middle of this leap that epistemology turns into ontology, problems of existence into issues of being, reasoning into power. And thus it is that both knowledge and power, resistance and legitimation, rest on a foundation of convention and agreement. The frightening alternative is madness, for Wittgenstein's remark cannot be repeated too often: "If I were sometime to see quite new surroundings from my window instead of the long familiar ones, if things, humans, and animals were to behave as they never did before, then I would say something like 'I have gone mad'; but that would merely be an expression of giving up the attempt to know my way about."

Does this mean that to be mad is to approach the limits of meaning? Perhaps! For in such situations I am left completely alone, for then I am not like anybody else; if "a" denotes myself, then there is no "b" to go with it. Not knowing my way about is another way of saying that I am completely lost, with no fixes to keep me steady, with no contexts to share. It is exactly at this moment of horror that the equal sign shows itself in its imperial nakedness; a blessing in disguise, an instrument of socialization, a standardized tool for making you and me normal, predictable, and interchangeable; logic is not merely a matter of form, even though the copula is the real subject of speculative thought.

The basic assumption of this reasoning mode is in the Leibnizian principle of salva veritatae; truth is preserved when two propositions are interchangeable in every context. Put differently, what I say about an object is assumed to be true regardless of what the object is called. In reality, however, two contexts are never exactly the same, for then there would not be two contexts but one. Likewise, two synonyms are never totally overlapping. My credibility is therefore a function of how I distinguish one context from another and of how I name the resulting categories. As expected, this is a privilege held by God himself. Let there be! And there was!

Even the naming is nameable. And this possibility poses again the Epimenidean question of whether a particular Order of Context is to be trusted. Is God—the key figure of power—logical? Is God himself true to the principles of salva veritatae and to the laws of consistency that are symbolized by the equal sign? Of course not! Especially in the Old Testament, God instead exercises his power by creating paradoxes, predicaments, and double binds; first he demands obedience and then he changes his commands. Abraham provides the paradigmatic case, and this is why he was so crucial both to Søren Kierkegaard and to Franz Kafka. But the man in question was already ninety-nine years old, when the Lord made the covenant with him that he was to be the father of a multitude of nations. This altered context was then codified in a decree that proclaimed that his name be changed from Abram to Abraham. New worlds require new labels, for what is true about an object is not independent of what it is called.

But the story continues. Genesis 22. The Almighty designs a test of Abraham's obedience. As a sign, he must sacrifice Isaac, his only son, whom he loves. No regrets, everything ready, the son tied to the altar, the knife on his throat. Then, suddenly, from the sky, the voice of the Lord's angel: "Stop! Stop! For Heaven's sake. Don't kill. Your master knows that you fear him. He changes his mind." The murder was no longer necessary, for in everything Abraham had already demonstrated his submission. Yet it was at this very moment of apparent relief that Abraham experienced limitless terror. God—the incarnation of power—is not to be trusted, for if he has changed his mind once, he can do so again. Only logic is predictable and God is not logical. Indeed "God" is nothing but a proper name for everything we sense is too important to ignore and too evasive to specify. "God" is a pseudonym of power.

To logic, paradox is an enemy; to power, predicament is an ally. Later dictators have become experts in the same form of institutionalized double bind and uncertainty. The torturer who by mistake kills his victim has eliminated this sense of uncertainty and thereby the whole point of his business; the torture is for the audience, not for the victim. The only defense may indeed be in the deployment of irony, satire, humor, and poetry; even though revolt is often necessary but ineffectual, refusal is always possible and irritating. As a consequence, dictators fear laughter more than tears, lonely poets more than organized protesters, happiness more than sorrow. But whereas humor and poetry engage in a play of logical types, deduction is characterized by consistency and a form of reasoning that moves from an axiomatic beginning to an inevitable end. Under the pressure of salva veritatae, even the equal sign transforms itself into an arrow, the key symbol of mimetic desire.

The best example is of course in the causal model. Here the equal sign serves as a selective filter that lets through more influences in one direction than in the other. At the same time, causal relations are often dressed up as logical relations, even though the two types of implication are drastically different; whereas cause-and-effect involves time, power, and responsibility, logic is without time, without freedom, and without guilt. In both cases, however, the argument strives for acceptance, for like all philosophy also logic is inherently rhetorical; the trick is to be believed, to reason in a manner that increases one's credibility. Belief is the instrument of power par excellence.

In this context, the most interesting rhetorical trope is the metonymy. Its strategy is to create trust by making the reader or listener recognize himself; its tactic is to let the concrete rule over the abstract, the specific over the general. This practice is itself part of the metaphysics of presence that permeates all empiricism. There is a high correlation between credibility and concretization, power and thingification, order and communication; the anatomy of power says that the way to the mind goes via the body, that discipline is anchored in details. Privilege and exploitative power have always masked themselves as duty and responsibility.

Perhaps there is nothing more powerful than the power of the example; speech is not only indicative but also imperative. The current challenge is to subvert that power. Indeed I have come to believe that our very survival depends upon improved abilities to be abstract enough; the most radical point is the point of insolvability. And with this call to abstractness I have already begun to move from the ordering parallels of the equal sign to the devious slant of the slash.

●　　●　　●

As the equal sign belongs to logic, so the slash stems from dialectics. While the former dominates positive science, the latter permeates deconstruction. It is in the former to symbolize knowledge as the restatement of identities, in the latter to denote the inseparability of identity and difference. The former searches for the certain in the ambiguous, the latter for the ambiguous in the certain.

Even though the two tropes are thoroughly intertwined, the equal sign gets its convincing power mainly from metonymy, the slash mainly from metaphor. It follows that the equal sign points the way to standardization and thingification, whereas the slash eludes all attempts to catch it. In both cases, however, the structures of substitution reflect the forms of power and the forms of power the structures of substitution. The ensuing problem has its roots in Plato: what makes us see must itself be invisible, what makes us understand must itself be nonunderstandable; the mirror is a mirror not for the mirrored but for the mirroring, not for the object in front of the glass but for the tain behind it. It is with the writings of Jacques Derrida that the discussion now is returning to a level of abstractness worthy of Hegel, Kant, and Descartes: What is reflection and what makes reflection possible? What can I know about what, except that epistemology never left the mirror stage and that thirsting for knowledge is an instance of unquenchable narcissistic desire?

It is this desire for the invisible that itself becomes visible in the slash, for to me the slanting line serves as a concrete symbol of an abstract relation; with T. S. Eliot, I conceive of symbols as objective correlates of human feelings. This may sound as if I try to reenlist the forces of metonymy, but then I seek consolation in Jacques Lacan's observation that the symbol manifests itself as the killing of the thing. Lacan's remark is important, because it is the very essence of a relation to be extremely abstract, invisible and untouchable; like silence, every attempt to capture it fails, for every attempt destroys it. It follows that relations cannot be defined, only experienced. Relations should not be confused with what is related, just as the desire for love should not be confused with the loved one.

Through the slash everything hangs together with everything else in a maze of internal and self-referential relations. Even algebra may serve as an example, for three times three would not be nine unless three times seven were twenty-one and seven times seven forty-nine. And so it is easier to understand both why dialectics has been called the algebra of revolution and why all revolutions fail. The concept of implication is a subjunctive that in empirical operationalization is perverted into an indicative. In the need to speak there is nevertheless a desire to silence, an idea of infinity, a sense of neither identity nor difference. The future is future because it is ungraspable, not because it is manipulable.

It follows that dialectics is not a predictive mode of reasoning or a metonymic system of causal models. It is rather a form of epistemology specialized in the discovery of the hidden in the apparent. As a consequence, it can never look into the future, only into the past, an insight that was born with Hegel, lived with Kierkegaard, and died with Stalin: dialectics is not a language of commands but a language of understanding, especially of the relations between repression and submission, master and slave.

The dialectic nature of the slash becomes especially evident in confrontations between the individual self on the one hand and the collective taken-for-granted on the other. Thus there are many who are shocked when they experience how society issues orders that to them seem unfair, or how it makes claims that to them are false. In these situations, the analyst usually asks whether he should put more trust in the individual or in the collective. The dialectician instead answers that neither is to be trusted, for the two words are defined in terms of one another and are hence in constant and unresolvable conflict.

It is nevertheless the void between individual and society that constitutes the realm of political power. The deep insights that fill this social space of silence must not be revealed, just as God the Father could not permit his children to eat from the tree of knowledge or to mention his name. It is indeed through the automatic recital of Commandments that society protects itself from its members and individuals guard against the collective. It is this that the slash symbolizes, that which the angels fear: relations beyond the related.

But how can I know that I as a subject conceive of the world in the same fashion as you do as an object? Assuming that this question lacks an answer (for there is no Other of the Other), by which right do you then engage in political action, an activity that in practice always means that the will of the Other is subordinated to your own? Is sociality to desire your neighbor? If so, how do you handle the problem that the collective "we" never can be anything but a majority; "social democracy" is an oxymoron. If the personal is political, then perhaps the political is pathological. For how small must a minority be before it is forbidden? And how large must a majority be before it becomes such an integral part of the taken-for-granted that it turns silent? For the State to wither away, it must be everywhere. Fascism is a tendency to homogeneity. After Gulag and Auschwitz critical thought can be nothing but Plural.

Political power is structured as a slash: internal, self-referential, insatiable as the silence of desire itself. Of all political concepts, intentionality is the most central and the least understood. Thingification is the price we pay for not accepting that there is a beyond beyond the beyond of expression, an absence inscribed without a trace in every discourse. The slash tries to be a symbol of this excluded third, which is neither either-or nor both-and, but something entirely outside the realm of naming; the slash is not what it first might have seemed—a bridge between opposites—but the void of categorical limits itself. And through the silence breaks the voice of Samuel Beckett's Unnamable (*Beckett Trilogy*, p. 352): "perhaps that's what I feel, an outside and an inside and me in the middle, perhaps that's what I am, the thing that divides the world in two, on the one side the outside, on the other the inside, that can be as thin as foil, I'm neither one side nor the other, I'm in the middle, I'm the partition, I've two surfaces and no thickness, perhaps that's what I feel, myself vibrating, I'm the tympanum, on the one hand the mind, on the other the world, I don't belong to either."

And so it is that the slash perhaps can serve as the signifier of that constellation in which nothing takes place except the place. Maybe it is even at this Mallarméan place of silence that truth and power hold their secret meetings. To stave off all trespassing into this sanctuary, God himself spoke these words to Moses, for him to bring down to the priests and the people (Exodus 20:4–6): "You shall not make for yourself a graven image, or any likeness of anything that is in heaven or above, or that is in the earth beneath, or that is in the water under the earth; for I the Lord your God am a jealous God, visiting the iniquity of the fathers upon the children to the third and the fourth generation of those who hate me, but showing steadfast love to thousands of those who love me and keep my commandments."

And so it is that issues of representation and the sublime may have more to do with ethics than with logics and aesthetics. Power is structured as a knowledge: "And the Lord said to Moses, 'Go down and warn the people, lest they break through to the Lord to gaze and many of them perish' " (Exodus 19:21). And in doing as he was told, Moses became the first politruk. The eye shows itself to be more powerful than the voice, the gaze more violent than the word.

• • •

Inherent in the issues of representation is a heightened awareness of the fundamental difference between word and object. This awareness is itself a part of that crisis of the sign which became acute in the second half of the nineteenth century, especially with writers like Baudelaire, Rimbaud, and Mallarmé. Once again, these artists were driven by a desire for the words they did not possess. In realizing that every utterance by necessity is indirect, they experienced how conventional language did not furnish the means to express what they most urgently wanted to express. Even when they said "stone" and meant "stone," they were not stone. Even when they said "you" and meant "you," they were not you. One can share what one has, not what one is. As a speaking subject, I have no choice but to live in a language that is common and social. The limits of my language mean the limits of my world.

It is this unfathomable problem of representation that to me finds an objective correlate in the Saussurean bar, i.e., in that horizontal line that simultaneously splits and unites the two fractions of the sign of

$$\frac{S}{s}$$

where "S" stands for "signifier" and "s" for "signified."

It is of course tempting to tie the capital S to the touchable physicality of the sign and the small s to its nontouchable meaning. Such an interpretation would be a serious oversimplification, however, for signs are always threaded together into braids of desire and justification. In a rhythmic dance of creativity, nominator and denominator constantly change positions.

Illustrations of such turnabouts are already in the *Odyssey*, especially in Odysseus's tale of how he was caught in the Cyclopes' cave (Ninth Song). When Polyphemos demanded the name of the intruder, he got the answer Ovtis, *Nohbdy*. The beast in turn replied that "Nohbdy the last one will be that I eat," upon which he fell asleep, full of red wine and human meat. It was at this crucial moment that the trickster saw his opportunity, rammed the red-hot pike of an olive tree into the drunkard's eye, leaned on it, and turned it as a shipwright turns a drill. And the pierced eyeball hissed broiling and the roots popped. The Cyclops howled in pain, and when his likes gathered outside the cave to learn what was wrong, Polyphemos roared in reply: "Nohbdy, Nohbdy's tricked me, Nohbdy's ruined me!" To this his friends responded: "Ah well, if nobody has played you foul there in your lonely bed, we are no use in pain given by great Zeus." And Odysseus was filled with laughter to see how like a charm the name deceived them.

Thus sounds the original tale of the crisis of the sign, of power structured as a knowledge, of identity statements as lies, of thingification and the sense of meaning. But this ur-tale has interesting connections also with the Greek concept of mimesis and thereby both with postmodernism and with René Girard. Inherent in this notion is the idea that art is an imitation—a re-pre-sentation—of reality. But neither the true artist nor the hegemonic ruler is satisfied with the mere copying of the outer appearance of a phenomenon. They also wish to touch its inner soul. Only with the sublime do they become full-fledged forgers. The bar eliminated, word and object united, mimetic desire completed.

Constitutive of the concept of mimesis is the assumption of a privileged original, a Holy Script, a Book of Nature. With this text as a starting point, the truth-teller's task is to provide a perfect translation, a mirror image, a narcissistic reflection. At the same time, I have already noted that perfect translation is impossible. The supplementary nature of language in fact implies that any reference to an original is highly misleading; the copy is not a copy of an original but a simulacrum, a copy that lacks an original. The Book of Nature is itself a simulacrum. As such it is untranslatable.

And thus it must be repeated: meaning does not emerge from the identity of signifier and signified, but from the difference between them. Indeed it is difference alone that allows a signifier to signify. Without signs no thoughts, without splits no signs. Referring to a once-and-for-all beginning is therefore not to refer at all, for without tenses and cases we would be literally lost. It follows that the ideal of total and perfect representation does not guarantee the stability of truth. Instead it vouches for its indeterminacy.

Filling the ontological gap between signifier and signified is the Saussurean Bar of Power. But whereas power is power because it transforms categories, analysis is analysis because it keeps them apart. As a consequence, the ——— can function not only as the wand of the ruler but also as the crowbar of the critic. This explains why also Marxian thought may be considered an early response to the crisis of the sign; the use-value of the commodity corresponds to the signifier, the exchange-value to the signified. To fetishize is in fact to see only the physical and be blind to its meaning; in reality, though, a commodity is a very queer thing abounding in metaphysical subtleties and theological niceties. No society can do without its religion of ontological transformations.

Similar attitudes permeate the theories of psychoanalysis and the practices of psychotherapy. Since the unconscious after Lacan is structured as a language, human crisis can be interpreted as a crisis of the sign, more specifically a crisis locatable to the bar. The therapeutic strategy is first to discover a repressed signified and then to kill it with an explicit signifier. The patient speaks herself well, for, in the powerfilled act of naming, anguish becomes graspable. The horrible and noncommunicable loses its frightening grip once it is caught in shared categories and domesticated in common expressions. Desire is tamed when subverted into desired; the phallus becomes a symbol of lack, desire thingified. Penis envy speaks clearly, the castration complex as well. But just as Saussure's bar blocks the road to the fulfillment of desire, so the way to self-understanding always goes via the Other. Fort-da. Fort-da. Fort-dada. But what does a woman want? What does it mean to be a woman in an age of iconography, at once a reflexive consciousness and a social product?

Here, as before, the processes of thingification and alienation seem to be governed by a mimetic desire. This drift to imitation expresses itself less in metaphoric condensations and more in metonymic displacements. It lies within René Girard's theory that we are striving to make signifier and signified into doubles of one another. But when this desire approaches satisfaction, the search for identity turns back on itself and changes into hostility. The desire can be kept alive only through the sacrifice of one of the antagonists. A scapegoat is selected, burdened with the collective guilt, and driven out of the community.

To me, the scapegoat carries many of the same traits as the rejected hypothesis, the power of the example, the prohibition against graven images. The desire is a desire for perfect communication, a desire impossible to satisfy. Put differently: power is a desire, not a need. It is this desire that I have symbolized as lines of power. It is the truth of this desire that no ruler can bear to hear.

●   ●   ●

And now, toward the end of the beginning, it should be clear what fascinates me. It is that strange transition point at which the light or sound waves of my textual performance hit your eyes or ears, move into the gray substance inside your head, stir around and become meaningful words, powerful enough to change both our understanding and our action. This abstract penumbra is to me in the intersection of a set of lines, all of which serve as condensations of knowledge, hence of communication. It is not sufficient to say how something is, I must also be believed when I say it. This is not to argue, however, that anything goes. On the contrary, for to be believed is to tread a dance with the taken-for-granted. To be believed is to have power. Power is almighty, the apparatchik its prophet. Not to philosophize is still to philosophize. Power is a desire to control meaning. The prime symbol of meaning is the copula IS, a verb designating an event.

Finally: Is this geography? Of course it is! For what is geography, if it is not the drawing and interpretation of lines. The only quality that makes my geography unusual is that it does not limit itself to the study of visible things. Instead it tries to foreshadow a cartography of thought. To practice this art, however, is incredibly difficult, for any attempt must face the challenge of being abstract enough.

In this context, it is with some dismay that I note how my thoughts of power have been unthinkable without the correlates of the straight lines. Even though this technique of fixing ideas is a minimalist approach, it is an approach nevertheless. But how do I write a theory à la Brancusi, a theory in which form and content are indistinguishable? And how do I practice a writing à la Beckett, in which I do not write *about* something, but in which the writing *is* that something itself? Mallarmé's example was to paint not the thing but the effect it produces.

Perhaps I enter this social space of silence by living in the world as I found it. A world where the unconscious is structured as a language, a world where power is structured as a knowledge, a world where lines are taken to their limits.

Mondrian.

All these words, all these strangers, this dust of words, with no
ground for their settling, no sky for their dispersing, coming together
to say, fleeing one another to say, that I am they, all of them, those
that merge, those that part, those that never meet, and nothing else,
yes, something else, that I'm something quite different, a quite
different thing, a wordless thing in an empty place, a hard shut dry
cold black place, where nothing stirs, nothing speaks, and that I
listen, and that I seek, like a caged beast born of caged beasts born of
caged beasts born of caged beasts born in a cage and dead in a cage,
born and then dead, born in a cage and dead in a cage, in a word like
a beast, in one of their words, like such a beast.

Samuel Beckett, *The Unnamable,* p. 356

Squaring

Maidens with squares
And compasses, watching over
The celestial blackboards.

And the angel of numbers,
Pensive, flying
From 1 to 2, from 2
To 3, from 3 to 4.

Cold chalks and sponges
Crossed out and erased
The light of the spaces.

Nor sun, moon, nor stars,
Nor the sudden green
Of the sunbeam and the lightning
Nor the air. Only clouds.

Maidens without squares,
Without compasses, weeping.

And on the dead blackboards,
The angel of numbers,
Without life, shrouded,
Over the 1 and the 2,
Over the 3, over the 4.

Rafael Alberti, *The Angel of Numbers,*
trans. C. M. Bowra

There is this mysterious blending of the familiar and the different. Recollections of shared memories. Anticipations of understandings. Yet another exercise in the art of self-conscious reevaluation. Minimum effort for maximum result.

A map of an intellectual odyssey of a man without qualities. Thirty years of roaming around concentrated into four points of intersecting lines. Forms of thought turned into thoughts of form, workings of the mind translated into a cartography of understanding. The point of one thought-position connected through lines with that of another, marks drawn on the dematerialized surface of a basic plane.

●

The journey can be pictured as the union of two Malevich squares, one on top of the other

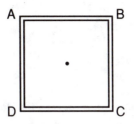

When the sides of the squares are horizontal and vertical, the figures are mute. Then, in the creative moment of operationalization, they suddenly turn in an ecstatic angle around their common center of indifference.

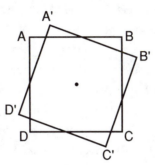

An irregular octagon is created as these points are connected by lines of philosophical development

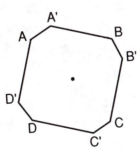

It was Kasimir Malevich who once wrote that "the square is a newly born, living and majestic, the first step of artistic creation." What now

remains is for me to take the next step. To do so, I must first assign proper names to the corners and connecting lines and then convince you that these names can serve as acceptable definite descriptions. For a summary see the figures at the end of this chapter.

●

The opening through which I thrust into the new space is at point **A.** This point I hereby baptize as human **ACTION.**

This is the same entrance through which I myself came into academic life toward the end of the 1950s. For a Swede of my generation this was the most natural choice, for written into the taken-for-granted was the imperative that the future should be made to be better than the past. The vehicle for reaching this utopian goal was to be **SCIENCE,** the name I therefore give to the activity located at point **B** of my figure.

The baseline of the Malevich square is consequently in the ethical connection between points **A** and **B,** i.e., in the joining together of the goals of action and the means of science. The arranged marriage was to be between the good and the true. Give me a firm leverage and I shall move the world!

It was through social engineering that abstract theory was to merge with concrete practice. Just as our laws of physical gravity had enabled us to construct airplanes that could fly and bridges that could stand, so the analogy was that laws of social gravity should enable us to construct a human world of justice and efficiency. The key to the future lay in the specification of invariant relations between cause and effect. Put differently, the world should be translated into the language of

$$y = f(x)$$

or be caught in the coordinate net of horizontal and vertical axis.

It is exactly here that something decisive occurs. To begin to speak, the horizontal base line **AB** must be tilted. Such a tilt is achieved through the mistranslation inherent in all operationalization. The point **A** consequently flips over into **A'** as human action finds its objective correlate in the symbol

Through this reformulation, it becomes obvious where the nucleus of Swedish ideology is located. It is in the origo, in the point at which the axes cross. Indeed, it is always in points of intersecting lines that genuine understanding is concentrated. Only such points are worthy of study.

To lure reality into the net of causal analysis, it must be called by its own name. Sirens sing. And with what better names could a budding geographer enchant reality than with those of "distance" and "human interaction." What a beautiful catch it was, that day when the world was pictured as a straight regression line, i.e., as

$\log I_{ij}$

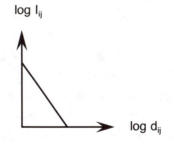

$\log d_{ij}$

or, in another language,

$$\log I_{ij} = a - b \log d_{ij}$$

The understanding of the world is here condensed into the two parameters a and b, i.e., into the two points at which the regression line and the axes intersect; the original data of human behavior reduced to its geographical essence. Perhaps it is the unconscious memory of this picture that now resurfaces in the ordering of the present volume itself; it is in the compositions of Piet Mondrian that I catch a glimpse of the aesthetics of thought.

Still. Knowledge is not only an issue of the aesthetics of form but also of the suspicion of hermeneutics. Could reality really be as well behaved as some of the early analyses indicated? Settling the doubt requires systematic studies of the parameter values, especially of how the b-values vary over time and space. In the squeezing of equations, the maximalism of data collection transcends itself into a minimalism of thought. It cannot be stressed too often: To understand and to create is not to have an idea that searches for its expression, but to have an expression that searches for its meaning.

And when the gravity expressions were sufficiently squeezed, the meanings began to shift. Not only did the world come out as more varied and erratic than it had first appeared. In addition, and more important, the squeezing changed the problem. What had begun as a study of human interaction indeed turned out to be a study of the spatial distribution of opportunities; the a- and b-values were not descriptions of human interaction per se, but instead the map of origins and destinations translated into another language. And this map itself was not a representation of points and lines but of a basic plane. What the gravity model had captured was not human behavior but the structure of a spatial prison. Caught in invisible chains, you imagine that you go to bed with a charming girl only to realize that you wake up with your own mother.

But wait! Who was my mother? What are action, science, and social engineering? Which are the reasoning rules that determine whether a statement is true or false? Were my conclusions valid or merely the effects of a particular mode of thought and justification? At any rate, the Swedish experiments led to more questions than answers. In the process of self-conscious reevaluation, the task of changing the world first turned into the problem of understanding the world, and then into that of understanding the understanding. The activity that was supposed to put the world on its feet was turned on its head.

•

To make it break into speech, the concept of **SCIENCE** must be further condensed. Point **B** must be flipped over into the operationalization of **B′**. But where is the pivotal idea of science? In my mind, it is concentrated into the word IS, now symbolized by the two lines of the equal sign

$$=$$

It is this sign that for me captures scientific knowledge in its purest, most abstract form. In essence, knowledge is the power of saying that something is something else and being believed when you do so. This is the problem of identity. How do I recognize something when I see it again? Easy to ask, difficult to answer. Dangerous to contemplate.

The standard approach is an application of the Leibnizian principle of salva veritatae. To recall once more, this principle says that truth is preserved when two propositions are interchangeable in every context. A rose is a rose is a rose. But the very point of this quote from Gertrude Stein was of course that it is *not* the case that a rose is a rose is a rose. In reality, two contexts are never exactly the same; there is nothing like a perfect synonym, not even anything like a perfect tautology. The credibility of my reformulations is therefore a function of how well I distinguish one context from another and of how successful I am in getting my labels accepted. Let there be! And this time there was *not*. For once, enough of repetitions! And thus it is that the equal sign appears as a blessing in disguise, not only as a powerful tool of socialization but also as a source of heresy. Conventional science is a church founded on a particular doctrine of identity. Theses, theses on the door, coming, coming more and more.

As an illustration, yet another anecdote. True and profoundly revolting.

The year was 1968. My friends kept talking about Karl Marx. Driven by a mimetic desire, I started to read him as well. I read once and understood not a word that I read. I tried again. Again and again. And then, suddenly, I understood what I did not understand: Marx's definition of the equal sign was drastically different from what I had been taught and had hitherto taken for granted. Even such a central word as "Capital" itself had one meaning on page 37, another on page 180, a third of page 306. Not because the text was badly written, but because the phenomenon under discussion changed as the story proceeded. Once more: How do I recognize something when I see it again, especially if it disguises itself under a set of aliases? The world is batlike, so even when I think that I see either a bird or a mouse, I must always remember that in fact it is a bat. A rose is a rose is a symbol of love. A symbol is a sign of shared beliefs. Rrose Sellavy, as Marcel Duchamp used to call it. Culture is a technique of categorization, a rhetorical ingredient in that ethical glue that keeps you and me simultaneously separated and united.

The confrontation between the Leibnizian and the Hegelian conceptions of identity brought a new and challenging issue into focus: Any technique for recognizing something again is itself a reflection of how I conceive the relations between word and object. In the tension between these two entities, should I put more trust in the former or in the latter? Not so easy, especially as I believe that whatever I happen to say tells more about the language I am speaking *in* than about the phenomena I am speaking *about*.

This belief has itself grown out of the Cartesian attitude that there are two kinds of phenomena, one of existence, the other of subsistence. Thus we can easily agree that the stone that now sits on my writing table is the same as the one I picked up fifteen years ago on the faraway shores of the Tasman Sea. It is more difficult to determine whether it also contains the same hopes and fears. For just as the rose is not merely a rose, so this little stone is not merely a stone. At the same time, it is also a symbol, a material expression of friendship and human relations. In its dematerialized form, the white stone is in effect a social artifact full of obligations and excuses, of joy and sadness, of guilt and punishment. But meaning is always contextual; for you, my discussion has turned the stone into a repository of philosophical problems; for myself and for three others it means much more than that.

With this recognition, the odyssey takes yet another turn. Pushed downward, the identity problem of recognizing something again leaps into the existence problem of assuring that what I see is what you see as well. The trick is to be believed. And in science, a given statement carries high credibility if it is doubly anchored, first in the logical thoughts of consistency, and then in the empirical facts of the present.

This metaphysical braiding of epistemology and ontology leads to point **C.** It is at this corner of the Malevich square that problems of agreement become prominent. Put differently, this is the meeting point of one and many, hence of individual and society. I give it the name of **MYTH,** but it could equally well be called **POLITICS.**

This point is as always a limit. Like all limits it is taboo. But why would something be forbidden, if it were not because it is too important to know? And why should I devote my studies to something less important than I can imagine?

When tilted into its objective correlate, this desire for the nonmentionable occupies the corner **C′,** symbolized in the slanting line of

/

As the equal sign encapsulates the spirit of scientific explanation, so the slash is the penumbra of human wisdom. In the process, the symbol manifests itself as the killing of the thing, and this is why relations must never be confused with what is related. As already noted, the slash is a dematerialized substitute of that excluded third which is neither either-or nor both-and, and something entirely outside the realm of naming. The slash is not what it first might have appeared—a bridge between dialectical opposites—but the most threatening one can imagine—the void of categorical limits itself. Once again I call for Janus, more prominent for us than ever for the Romans: Help me become a sinner yet not lose my sanity!

Said! Perhaps shown. And exactly because power is a game of ontological transformations, so the rules of the game must be kept secret;

the magician performs his tricks, he does not give them away. Yet: to understand power the analyst must approach the forbidden boundary between individual and society. It is of this permeable limit that the slash is a graven image. Go down and warn the people lest they perish.

•

When these warnings are taken seriously, it becomes clear that the exercise of power is a form of **ART.** This is therefore the name I give to corner **D** of the Malevich square; even to Kant, imagination is the faculty of representation, of making present what is absent. When tilted into point **D′,** this faculty finds its symbol in the Saussurean bar of

———

It need not be repeated how it is in this line that I sense the membrane through which thing and meaning, word and object, begin to penetrate one another. It is in the desire of perfect communication that we strive to make signifier and signified into doubles. But it is also in the violence of this same drive that when it approaches satisfaction, then either the S or the s must be killed. If not, communication will turn into silence; the fraction between nominator and denominator equals one both for

$$\frac{S}{S}$$

and for

$$\frac{s}{s}$$

But even though this is the desired state, such a perfect sign could never communicate; it is well established that meaning stems from difference, not from identity.

It should nevertheless be noted that the silences of fraction 1 are of two kinds. When produced by the capital S the silence is that of idle chatter; when produced by the small s it is that of autism. The former exemplifies society conversing with itself. The latter is the individual refusing to be a part.

But how do I persuade others that this characterization of speech and silence offers insights into the art of power? Perhaps by recalling from the *Tractatus* (4.1212) that "what can be shown cannot be said."

Once here, it is tempting to imagine Aristotle as the legislator of what can be said and Euclid as the discoverer of what can be shown. Just as logic has its acceptable modes of reasoning, so geometry has its acceptable forms of demonstration. It is in this light that I interpret Euclid's sign-off signal "hoper edei," or "Quod Erat" as a mark of rhetorical distinction.

It should now be noted that Euclid used two different expressions to signify the successful end of a proof. One was the QED—Quod Erat Demonstrandum—the other the QEF—Quod Erat Faciendum. With the former, the persuasive power lies in the adherence to geometric reasoning. With the latter, it is in the practice of drawing lines. With the QED, the equivalence is in the intellectual mind; with the QEF, in the sensitive body. In the former, the line AB equals CD; in the latter, three feet in one direction measures the same distance as three feet in another. And thus it seems that proofs signed QEF carry a higher degree of credibility. Whenever in doubt, the body is the mind's corrective; to think is to say, to see is to show.

●

Therefore. As a way of connecting the Malevich points of **D** and **A,** I simply use yet another quote from Wittgenstein's *Tractatus* (6.421 and 6.43): "It is clear that ethics cannot be put into words. Ethics is transcendental. (Ethics and aesthetics are one and the same.) . . . The

world of a happy man is a different one from that of the unhappy man."
And thereby I return also to Malevich and his remark that "the square I
have exhibited is not an empty square, but the sensibility of the absence of
the object."

Such is the point of this line of thought.

●　　●　　●

Does it not follow, then, that, as for lovers the sight of the
beloved is the thing they love most, . . . so for friends the most
desirable thing is living together? For friendship is a partnership, and
as man is to himself, so he is to his friend. . . . Each class of men
wish to occupy themselves with their friends; and so some drink
together, others play dice together, others join in athletic exercises and
hunting, or in the study of philosophy, each class spending their days
together in whatever they love most in life . . . Thus the friendship of
bad men turns out an evil thing, while the friendship of good men is
good, being augmented by their companionship; and they are thought
to become better too by their activities and by improving each other;
for from each other they take the mould of the characteristic they
approve . . . So much, then, for friendship; our next task must be to
discuss pleasure.

Aristotle, *Nicomachean Ethics,* Book 9

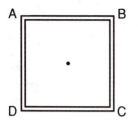

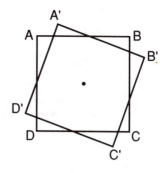

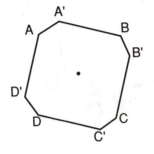

SPECIFICATION

A	Action	A′	**L**
B	Science	B′	=
C	Myth	C′	/
D	Arts	D′	——

AB	Ethics	A′B′	Epistemology
BC	Metaphysics	B′C′	Logic
CD	Ontology	C′D′	Dialectics
DA	Aesthetics	D′A′	Rhetoric

AA′	Good
BB′	True
CC′	Credible
DD′	Sublime

QEF

Squaring

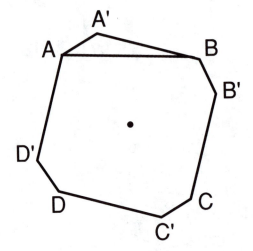

SPECIFICATION

A	Action	A'	**L**
B	Science	B'	=
C	Myth	C'	/
D	Arts	D'	——

AB	Ethics

AA'	Power	A'B'	Intentionality
BB'	Identity	B'C'	Categorization
CC'	Existence	C'D'	Being
DD'	Limit	D'A'	Representation

AC	Theory/Practice
BD	Paradox/Predicament

QED

Malevich Torpedoed

There is a double helix in the social sciences too.

•

Shot through the tube of ontological categorization comes a torpedo of power. At the center of this projectile is a turbo-prop engine designed according to the identity-difference principle of the equal sign. On each side of the parallel lines are forces of opposite modes of being. As these are turned on and off, the torpedo propels itself into the ontological transformations that constitute human action. It is the fluctuation between signifier and signified that gives rise to the spiraling movement of a double helix.

In the ethical operationalization of the $\llcorner$, the grenade sucks desire; in the dialectical indifference of the /, it spews castration. In the hole of point $\llcorner$, aesthetics is transformed into epistemology; in the void of $=$, epistemology turns to ontology; in the unnamable of /, ontology becomes metaphysics. Quod Erat Inveniendum.

●

Properly aimed, the torpedo may blow existence apart. Rescue operations, Red Cross missions. Gates closed. Diana at rest.

●

It is the gate-keeping duty of Janus to admit some conclusions and reject some others. Applying the stamp of QED is straightforward, because all it takes is a check that conventional reasoning rules have been followed. Employing the QEF requires more courage, for what is thereby accepted must be anchored in the body itself. Using the approval stamp of the QEI is so rare that it is almost incredible; the challenge is that when I look out of my window and see something I never saw before, then it is uncertain whether the signs reflect social things or solipsist mind. Out there, in here? You or I. Madness of Nowhere. Power stripped bare by her bachelors even: Quod Erat, "which was to be"; the panties of Demonstrandum, Faciendum, and Inveniendum whisked to the public.

Encore un coup de dés. Doubling the stakes, miming the twin. Dice rolling across the pages. Three. Two. One. Zero. Blast-off!

And yet. Whenever in doubt, merely note that in the act of reading these words, you thereby confirm that the points, lines, and planes are not mine alone. Perhaps they are what I sometimes believe: graven images of intimate communication.

●

And at the very moment that I saw the temple gates closing, they were suddenly thrown open again. What remains is nothing but a faint memory, an image blown away like the morning mist: Janus and Diana briefly caught in the middle of the act.

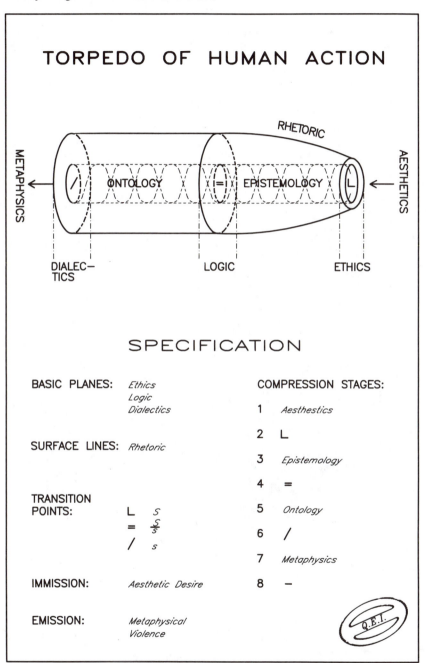

TORPEDO OF HUMAN ACTION

SPECIFICATION

BASIC PLANES:	*Ethics*	**COMPRESSION STAGES:**	
	Logic		
	Dialectics	1	*Aesthestics*
		2	L
SURFACE LINES:	*Rhetoric*	3	*Epistemology*
		4	=
TRANSITION POINTS:	L *s*	5	*Ontology*
	= $\frac{s}{\frac{s}{s}}$	6	/
	/ *s*	7	*Metaphysics*
IMMISSION:	*Aesthetic Desire*	8	–
EMISSION:	*Metaphysical Violence*		

Malevich Torpedoed

RESENTATION

Stately plump

Endings

There is a relation yet a distinction between what I say, what I say something about, and what I say about what I say something about. This mutual dependence is especially clear in the intertwining of epistemology and ontology: my knowledge of the world and my delimitation of the world are intimately connected.

The braiding of epistemology and ontology is inevitable, even though the former activity tends to dominate during some periods, the latter during some others. The transition from modernism to postmodernism provides a recent example of such a shift; whereas modernism deals primarily with epistemological questions of a relational nature, postmodernism experiments with ontological issues of fundamental importance. As modernism searches for purposeful answers to well-defined riddles, postmodernism explodes in cascades of paradoxical situations. The conscious colonizing of a world lost turns into aimless encounters with characters of doubtful existence. Paradigmatic cases of the former are in the detective story, the scientific/technological monograph, and the politics of social democracy; of the latter in science fiction, pataphysics, and anarchism.

Yet, there are no radical distinctions between modernism and postmodernism, merely a heightened awareness of the same crisis of the sign. This crisis became acute in the second half of the nineteenth century, especially with writers like Baudelaire, Rimbaud, and Mallarmé. Once again these artists were driven by a desire for the words they lacked. Since they realized that every utterance by necessity is indirect, they experienced how they were unable to express what they felt was most important to express. Postmodernism is in fact the culmination of modernism's assault on the idea of representation.

The distinctions between word and object, presence and absence, led to a deeper understanding of language and thereby to a poetry that explicitly tried to express the inexpressible. Thus I interpret postmodernism as an escalation of that desire for the different that is inherent already in modernism itself. All attempts to escape from the prison house of language turn back on themselves. As a speaking subject, I have no choice but to express myself in a language that is common and social. And thus it is that as modernism becomes postmodernism, the epistemological search for knowledge transcends itself into ontological issues of Being. And the prow sheared through the night and into the dawn.

•   •   •

Like many others, I have long read the major works of James Joyce — *Ulysses* and *Finnegans Wake* — as paradigmatic illustrations of the transition from modernism to postmodernism, from epistemology to ontology, from stable identities to shifting existences, from certainty to plurabilities. The well-known endings provide keys to a deeper understanding of human life in time and space.

The modernist *Ulysses* closes with a long internal monologue in which Molly Bloom remembers, suppresses, and distorts. In the borderland between being awake and asleep, her mind wavers between here and there, now and then. Yet it is not difficult to follow her, for even though she moves between contexts she remains always the same. Her monologue is clearly tied to her inner self, yet it is so general that the reader never gets lost. And then, toward the end, it comes, the solution to the riddle of who she is and of how she became who she is. The words are coherent, a stream from Molly's unconscious, not so difficult to translate into another language: "Och den natten vi missade båten vid Algericas vakten rörde sig fridfullt med sin lampa och O denna oemotståndliga ström O och havet havet som eld och de storslagna solnedgångarna och fikonträden i Alamedas trädgårdar ja alla de ringlande gränderna och husen de skära och blåa och gula och trosenträdgårdarna och pelargonierna och kaktusarna och Gibraltar som flicka där jag var en Bergsblomma ja när jag satte en ros i mitt hår som de andalusiska flickorna eller skall jag ta en röd och hur han kysste mig under den moriska muren och jag tänkte nå väl han så väl som nån ann och så bad jag honom med ögonen att be igen ja och så bad han ville jag ja säga ja min bergsblomma och först slog jag armarna om honom ja och drog honom till mig så han kände mina bröst all parfym ja och hans hjärta bankade vilt och ja sa jag ja jag vill Ja."

Nothing unusual about that. How many have not in their dreams heard the words, seen the eyes, felt the touch. But in the postmodern *Finnegans Wake* it is harder to determine what and who are the same, for the woman no longer carries the particular name of Molly Bloom but the general initials ALP—Anna Livia Plurabelle, the housewife Anna Livia, the river Liffey. What is rendered are not the specificities of an individual unconscious but fragments of a collective unconscious. The identities of ALP are radically indeterminate and this is why she is reunited with herself in new indeterminacy. The untranslatable ending: "and I rush, my only, into your arms. I see them rising! Save me from those therrble prongs! Two more. Onetwo moremens more. So. Avelaval. My leaves have drifted from me. All. But one clings still. I'll bear it on me. To remind me of. Lff! So soft this morning, ours. Yes. Carry me along, taddy, like you done through the toy fair! If I see him bearing down on me now under whitespread wings like he'd come from Arkangels, I sink I'd die down over his feet, humbly dumbly, only to washup. Yes, tid. There's where. First. We pass through grass

Endings

behush the bush to. Whish! A gull. Gulls. Far calls. Coming, far! End here.
Us then. Finn, again! Take. Bussoftlhee, mememormee! Till thousendsthee.
Lps. The keys to. Given! A way a lone a last a loved a long the
upon which the definite article returns without punctuation of its own volition
to the beginning found again, to the very first words of that book of books

  riverrun, past Eve and Adam's, from swerve of shore to bend of bay,
brings us by a commodius vicus of recirculation back to Howth Castle and
Environs."

  The female ALP reunited with the male HCE—Here Comes
Everybody, H. C. Earwicker, human erring and condonable. The double
anchor sunk into the ambiguous surfdom of complementarity. When Mrs.
Bloom and Anna Livia watch their men naked, they can no longer escape.
The verb "is"—the nucleus of knowledge—changes meaning with the
context. In radical postmodernism everything is genuinely indeterminable,
for both impressions and expressions are suspended in the abyss between
categories. Being approaches Nothingness as propositions of what is the
case pose questions of what there is. The contexts of words show
themselves to be as indeterminable as the words of context. Interpretation
is nevertheless authoritarian, for the greatest threat to knowledge has
always come from the undecidable.

In Parentheses

Adorno, Theodor W. *Negative Dialectics*. New York: Seabury Press, 1973. (German original, 1966.)

Alberti, Rafael. *Selected Poems*. Berkeley: University of California Press, 1966. (Spanish original, "El angel de los numeros," 1929.)

Aragon, Louis. *Paris Peasant*. London: Picador, 1988. (French original, 1924–25.)

Aristotle. *The Basic Works*. New York: Random House, 1941.

Asplund, Johan. *Det sociala livets elementära former*. Stockholm: Liber, 1983.

———. *Rivaler och syndabockar*. Göteborg: Korpen, 1989.

Austin, J. L. *How to Do Things with Words*. London: Oxford University Press, 1962.

Barthes, Roland. *Mythologies*. New York: Hill & Wang, 1972. (French original, 1957.)

———. *A Lover's Discourse: Fragments*. New York: Hill & Wang, 1978. (French original, 1977.)

Bataille, Georges. *The Story of the Eye*. Harmondsworth: Penguin, 1982. French quotations from *L'histoire de l'oeil*. Paris: Pauvert, 1979. (French original, 1928.)

———. *Visions of Excess: Selected Writings, 1927–1939*. Minneapolis: University of Minnesota Press, 1985.

Bateson, Gregory. *Mind and Nature: A Necessary Unity.* London: Wildwood House, 1979.

Beckett, Samuel. *Whoroscope.* Paris: Hours Press, 1930.

_____. *The Beckett Trilogy: Molloy, Malone Dies, The Unnamable.* London: Picador, 1979. (French originals, 1950–52.)

Beckett, Samuel, et al. *Our Exagmination Round His Factification for Incamination of Work in Progress.* Paris: Shakespeare and Company, 1929.

Bely, Andrei. *Petersburg.* Bloomington: Indiana University Press, 1978. (Russian original, 1916.)

Benjamin, Walter. *One Way Street and Other Writings.* London: New Left Books, 1979. (German originals, 1916–37.)

Berman, Marshall. *All That Is Solid Melts into Air.* New York: Simon & Schuster, 1982.

Bernstein, Richard. *Praxis and Action.* Philadelphiia: University of Pennsylvania Press, 1971.

Black, Max. *Models and Metaphors.* Ithaca, N.Y.: Cornell University Press, 1962.

Blanchot, Maurice. *Death Sentence.* Barrytown, N.Y.: Station Hill Press, 1978. (French original, 1948.)

Bourdieu, Pierre. *Outline of a Theory of Practice.* Cambridge: Cambridge University Press, 1977. (French original, 1972.)

Bowra, C. M. *The Creative Experience.* London: Macmillan, 1949.

Breton, André. *Manifestoes of Surrealism.* Ann Arbor: University of Michigan Press, 1969. (French original, 1924.)

_____. *Nadja.* New York: Grove Press, 1960. (French original, 1928.)

_____. *Mad Love.* Lincoln: University of Nebraska Press, 1987. (French original, 1937.)

Brown, Norman O. *Life Against Death.* Middletown, Conn.: Wesleyan University Press, 1959.

_____. *Closing Time.* New York: Vintage, 1974.

Bury, Pol. *Le sexe des anges et celui des géomètres.* Paris: Galilée, 1976.

Calvino, Italo. *Invisible Cities.* New York: Harcourt Brace Jovanovich, 1974. (Italian original, 1972.)

Canetti, Elias. *Crowds and Power.* New York: Viking Press, 1966. (German original, 1960.)

_____. *Kafka's Other Trial: The Letters to Felice.* Harmondsworth: Penguin, 1982 (German original, 1969.)

Carroll, Lewis. *The Annotated Alice.* New York: Clarkson N. Potter, 1960. (Originals, 1865–71.)

Cassirer, Ernst. *An Essay on Man.* New Haven: Yale University Press, 1944.

Certeau, Michel de. *The Practice of Everyday Life.* Berkeley: University of California Press, 1984.

Cixous, Hélène. "Castration or Decapitation?" *Signs* 7 (1981), 41–55.

Cixous, Hélène, and Catherine Clément. *The Newly Born Woman.* Minneapolis: University of Minnesota Press, 1986. (French original, 1975.)

Curry, Leslie. "The Random Economy: An Exploration in Settlement Theory." *Annals of the Association of American Geographers* 54 (1964), 138–46.

Davidson, Donald. *Inquiries into Truth and Interpretation.* Oxford: Clarendon Press, 1984.

de Man, Paul. *Allegories of Reading.* New Haven: Yale University Press, 1979.

Derrida, Jacques. *Of Grammatology.* Baltimore: The Johns Hopkins University Press, 1976. (French original, 1967.)

_____. *Spurs: Nietzsche's Styles/Éperons: Les styles de Nietzsche*. Chicago: University of Chicago Press, 1979.

_____. *Dissemination*. Chicago: University of Chicago Press, 1981. (French original, 1972.)

_____. *Margins of Philosophy*. Chicago: University of Chicago Press, 1982. (French original, 1972.)

_____. *Glas*. Lincoln: University of Nebraska Press, 1986. (French original, 1974.)

_____. *The Truth in Painting*. Chicago: University of Chicago Press, 1987. (French original, 1978.)

Dufy, Bruce. *The World as I Found It*. New York: Ticknor & Fields, 1987.

Dummett, Michael. *Frege: Philosophy of Language*. New York: Harper & Row, 1973.

Durkheim, Emile. *The Rules of Sociological Method*. New York: Free Press, 1964. (French original, 1895.)

Elias, Norbert. *The Civilizing Process*. New York: Urizen Books, 1978. (German original, 1939.)

Farinelli, Franco. *Pour une théorie générale de la géographie*. Geneva: Georythmes, no. 25, 1989.

Foucault, Michel. *The Order of Things*. New York: Vintage, 1973. (French original, 1966.)

_____. *Discipline and Punish*. New York: Pantheon, 1977. (French original, 1975.)

_____. *The History of Sexuality*. Harmondsworth: Penguin, 1981. (French original, 1976.)

_____. *Maurice Blanchot: The Thought from Outside*. New York: Zone Books, 1987. (French original, 1987.)

Freud, Sigmund. *Totem and Taboo*. London: Routledge & Kegan Paul, 1950. (German original, 1913.)

Gasché, Rodolphe. *The Tain of the Mirror: Derrida and the Philosophy of Reflection*. Cambridge, Mass.: Harvard University Press, 1986.

Gass, William H. *On Being Blue*. Boston: David R. Godine, 1977.

_____. *Fiction and the Figures of Life*. Boston: Nonpareil, 1979.

Geertz, Clifford. "Deep Play: Notes on the Balinese Cockfight." *Daedalus* 101 (Winter 1972), 1–37.

Giddens, Anthony. *The Constitution of Society*. Cambridge: Polity Press, 1984.

Girard, René. *Things Hidden Since the Foundation of the World*. Stanford: Stanford University Press, 1987. (French original, 1978.)

Habermas, Jürgen. *The Theory of Communicative Action*. London: Heinemann, 1984. (German original, 1981.)

d'Harnancourt, Anne, and Kynaston McShine, eds. *Marcel Duchamp*. New York: Museum of Modern Art, 1973.

Hartman, Geoffrey. *Saving the Text: Literature/Derrida/Philosophy*. Baltimore: The Johns Hopkins University Press, 1981.

Harvey, David. *Consciousness and the Urban Experience*. Oxford: Basil Blackwell, 1985.

Hegel, G. W. F. *Phenomenology of Spirit*. Oxford: Clarendon Press, 1977. (German original, 1807.)

Heidegger, Martin. *Being and Time*. New York: Harper & Row, 1962. (German original, 1927.)

Hemingway, Ernest. *Across the River and into the Trees*. New York: Charles Scribner's Sons, 1950.

Hintikka, Jaakko. *Models of Modalities*. Dordrecht: Reidel, 1969.

_____. *The Game of Language*. Dordrecht: Reidel, 1983.

Homer. *The Odyssey*. Trans. R. Fitzgerald. New York: Doubleday, 1963.

Horkheimer, Max, and Theodor W. Adorno. *Dialectic of Enlightenment*. New York: Seabury Press, 1972. (German original, 1944.)

Husserl, Edmund. *Cartesian Meditations*. The Hague: Martinus Nijhoff, 1973. (German original, 1929.)

Irigaray, Luce. *This Sex Which Is Not One*. Ithaca, N.Y.: Cornell University Press, 1985. (French original, 1977.)

Joyce, James. *Ulysses*. New York: Modern Library, 1934. (Original, 1922.)

———. *Finnegans Wake*. New York: Viking Press, 1959. (Original, 1939.)

Kandinsky, Wassily. *Concerning the Spiritual in Art*. New York: Dover, 1977. (German original, 1911.)

———. *Point and Line to Plane*. New York: Dover, 1979. (German original, 1926.)

Kant, Immanuel. *Critique of Pure Reason*. Garden City, N.Y.: Doubleday, 1966. (German original, 1781.)

———. *Critique of Practical Reason*. Chicago: University of Chicago Press, 1949. (German original, 1788.)

———. *Critique of Judgment*. New York: Hagner, 1951. (German original, 1790.)

Kripke, Saul A. *Wittgenstein on Rules and Private Language*. Oxford: Basil Blackwell, 1982.

Kristeva, Julia. "The Speaking Subject." In Marshall Blonsky, ed. *On Signs*. Oxford: Basil Blackwell, 1985.

Kyrklund, Willy. *Polyfem förvandlad*. Stockholm: Bonnier, 1964.

Lacan, Jacques. *Écrits: A Selection*. London: Tavistock, 1977. (French original, 1966.)

Lachterman, David Rapport. *The Ethics of Geometry*. New York: Routledge, 1989.

Lévi-Strauss, Claude. *The Raw and the Cooked*. New York: Harper & Row, 1969. (French original, 1964.)

Linde, Ulf. *Marcel Duchamp*. Stockholm: Rabén & Sjögren, 1986.

Linsky, Leonard. *Referring*. London: Routledge & Kegan Paul, 1967.

Machado, Antonio. *Times Alone: Selected Poems*. Middletown, Conn.: Wesleyan University Press, 1983. (Spanish original, "Anoche cuando dormía," 1902.)

Malevich, Kasimir. *Essays on Art*, vols. 1 and 2. Copenhagen: Borgen, 1968. (Russian originals, 1915–33.)

Mallarmé, Stéphane. *The Poems*. Harmondsworth: Penguin, 1977. (French original, "Un coup de dés," 1897.)

Marcuse, Herbert. *One-Dimensional Man*. Boston: Beacon Press, 1964.

Marx, Karl. *Grundrisse*. Harmondsworth: Penguin, 1973. (German notes, 1857–58.)

———. *Capital*. New York: International Publishers, 1967. (German original, 1867–94.)

Marx, Karl, and Friedrich Engels. *The German Ideology*. New York: International Publishers, 1947. (German original, 1846.)

Mauss, Marcel. *The Gift*. New York: Norton, 1967. (French original, 1925.)

Merleau-Ponty, Maurice. *The Visible and the Invisible*. Evanston, Ill.: Northwestern University Press, 1968. In Swedish partly as "Sammanflätningen-Kiasmen," *Kris* 31–32 (1985), 65–75. (French original, 1964.)

Monteiga, Robert C. *The Poetry of Rafael Alberti: A Visual Approach*. London: Támesis, 1978.

Musil, Robert. *The Man without Qualities*. London: Picador, 1979. (German originals, 1930–42.)

Nietzsche, Friedrich. *The Will to Power*. New York: Vintage, 1968. (German originals, 1883–88.)

———. *Thus Spoke Zarathustra*. Harmondsworth: Penguin, 1978. (German original, 1885.)

Ollman, Bertell. *Alienation: Marx's Conception of Man in Capitalist Society.* Cambridge: Cambridge University Press, 1971.

Olsson, Gunnar. *Birds in Egg/Eggs in Bird.* London: Pion, 1980.

Oxford English Dictionary, compact edition. Oxford: Oxford University Press, 1971.

Papageorgiou, Yorgo. *The Isolated City State.* London, Routledge, 1990.

Paz, Octavio. *Marcel Duchamp: Appearance Stripped Bare.* New York: Viking Press, 1978.

Pred, Allan. *Lost Words and Lost Worlds.* Cambridge: Cambridge University Press, 1989.

Quine, W. V. *Word and Object.* Cambridge, Mass.: MIT Press, 1960.

Rorty, Richard. *Philosophy and the Mirror of Nature.* Princeton: Princeton University Press, 1979.

Sartre, Jean-Paul. *Being and Nothingness.* New York: Washington Square Press, 1988. (French original, 1986.)

Saussure, Ferdinand de. *Course in General Linguistics.* London: Duckworth, 1983. (French notes, 1907–11.)

Searle, John R. *Speech Acts.* Cambridge: Cambridge University Press, 1969.

Sophocles. *The Oedipus Cycle.* Trans. D. Fitts and R. Fitzgerald. New York: Harcourt, Brace & World, 1939.

Staten, Henry. *Wittgenstein and Derrida.* Oxford: Basil Blackwell, 1985.

Stein, Gertrude. *The Autobiography of Alice B. Toklas.* New York: Harcourt, Brace, 1933.

Ulmer, Gregory L. *Applied Grammatology.* Baltimore: The Johns Hopkins University Press, 1985.

Valéry, Paul. *Selected Writings.* New York: New Directions, 1950. (French originals, 1927–47.)

Vico, Giambattista. *The New Science.* Ithaca, N.Y.: Cornell University Press, 1948. (Italian original, 1744.)

Whitehead, Alfred North, and Bertrand Russell. *Principia Mathematica.* Cambridge: Cambridge University Press, 1910–13.

Whitman, Walt. *Leaves of Grass.* New York: New American Library, 1955. (Original deathbed edition, 1892.)

Wittgenstein, Ludwig. *Tractatus Logico-Philosophicus.* London: Routledge & Kegan Paul, 1961. (Bilingual original, 1922.)

_____. *Philosophical Investigations.* Oxford: Basil Blackwell, 1953.

_____. *Zettel.* Oxford: Basil Blackwell, 1967. (Original fragments, 1929–48.)

_____. *Culture and Value.* Oxford: Basil Blackwell, 1980. (Original remarks, 1914–51.)

von Wright, Georg Henrik. *Explanation and Understanding.* Ithaca, N.Y.: Cornell University Press, 1971.

Beginnings

The present volume is a retrospective of self-portraits. With one crucial exception, the chapters stem from the decade around 1984. They were retouched and put together on the island of Sicily in the summer of 1990. Never was there a vacation more recreative, never a merger more complete. Birgitta was with me. Ulrika paid a visit.

Each portrait has its own story. Every reporter knows that if you want to make something up, you must be very precise.

I

The two introductions "Nowhere" and "Dematerialized" were written where the fire of Etna meets the water of the Ionian. The words of W.K. are quotes from Wassily Kandinsky's *Point and Line to Plane* originally published in 1926. Kandinsky's work has contributed immensely to my own self-understanding and the GO thereof. Yet, it had no influence on the initial formulations, for it was not until May of 1990 that I read it.

L

"Sermon of Remembrance" has its roots in "Toward a Sermon of Modernity," originally published in Mark Billinge, Derek Gregory, and Ron Martins, eds., *Recollections of a Revolution: Geography as Spatial Science* (London: Macmillan, 1984). What is included here is a heavily reworked and adjusted version of the original. The latter was written in the evening of June 1, 1980, in the bar of the Helsinki airport. On my way from St. Petersburg, I remembered

and forgot. In the process, I forged a new conscience.

The first figure of the TEXT is an adaptation of Constantin Brancusi's "Symbol of Joyce." When John Joyce saw it for the first time, he remarked: "The boy seems to have changed a good deal."

"Creativity and Socialization" is a rewriting of "Of Creativity and Socialization," *Archivio Studi Urbani e Regionale* 14 (1983), 143–54. It condenses a theme more fully developed in *Birds in Egg/Eggs in Bird* (London: Pion, 1980). The original article plays an important role in my own biography, for it was the afterbirth of my first lecture tour to Italy. I did not know it at the time, but now I realize how deeply my Latin friends have touched me; as children they were taught those classical paradoxes that I have had to learn on my own.

=

"On Doughnutting" is an abbreviation of a discussion with the same title from Sture Allén, ed., *Possible Worlds in Humanities, Arts and Sciences: Proceedings of Nobel Symposium 65* (Berlin: Walter de Gruyter, 1989). The original was an invited response to the paper "Exploring Possible Worlds" by Jaakko Hintikka, included in the same proceedings. The exchange occurred in Stockholm in August of 1986.

"Magician's Wand" is a modification of the lecture "Human Action as Magician's Tricks," presented in Milan, April 1987, as part of the series Frontiere della Scienza e della Tecnologia, sponsored by the Montedison Progetto Cultura. An Italian translation is included as a chapter of my *Linee senza ombre* (Roma: Edizione Theoria, 1991).

"Set Your Mind at Rest" was written in Ann Arbor in the summer of 1974. It is lifted directly from *Birds in Egg/Eggs in Bird.* Of all my writings none has influenced me more.

/

"Hazerdous Hazard" appeared originally under the rubric "-/-". It grew out of a small meeting of like-minded geographers sponsored by the Rockefeller Foundation and held at the Villa Serbelloni in August 1980. Together with other contributions to the same event, it was included in Peter Gould and Gunnar Olsson, eds., *A Search for Common Ground* (London: Pion, 1982).

"Social Space of Silence" is a shortened edition of "The Social Space of Silence," *Society and Space* 5 (1987), 249–62. This collage was finished in Sweden in the summer of 1984, submitted for publication, and promptly turned down. Three years later, the rejecting journal came back and asked for it. The history of postmodernism is itself postmodern. Silentium!

—

"The Eye and the Index Finger" is a reformulation of "The Eye and the Index Finger: Bodily Means to Cultural Meaning," in Reginald Golledge, Helen Couclelis, and Peter Gould, eds., *A Ground for Common Search* (Santa Barbara: Santa Barbara Geographical Press, 1988). It was first performed at a theater festival in Copenhagen in June 1985 and then again at a colloquium on geographical imagination held at the University of Geneva in October 1985.

"Hooked" is a translation of the Swedish newspaper report "Blodets rytm, strändernas svall," *Expressen,* July 6, 1985.

"Hemming the Way" is a touch-up of "The Language of Geography and the Geography of Language," in Gabriel Zanetto, ed., *Les langages des représentations geographiques* (Venice: EST Edizioni, 1989). It builds on a lecture presented in October 1987, first at the conference of German-speaking geographers in Munich, then at a colloquium of French and Italian geographers in Venice.

☐

"Lines of Power" is a paper of the same title printed in Trevor Barnes and James S. Duncan, eds., *Writing Worlds* (London: Routledge, 1991). It is a condensed variation on the theme of "Mödom mod och morske män," in Yvonne Hirdman, ed., *Maktens former* (Stockholm: Carlsson, 1989), completed in the fall of 1988 as part of the Swedish State Investigation Into Power. The English version stems from a paper delivered at the annual meetings of the Association of American Geographers, Baltimore, April 1989.

"Squaring" is a written version of "Forms of Thought," originally presented in April 1990 as the sixth annual Reginald Golledge lecture at the University of California, Santa Barbara. As always, I appreciated the friendship and the pleasure, the stones, the oysters, and the Chardonnays. And Ylva was a joy.

"Malevich Torpedoed" hit the writing pad on Sunday, July 29, 1990, at a sidewalk table on Piazza del Popolo in Rome. It was the tangible outcome of an immaculate conception at which Ole Michael Jensen had played the role of the archangel. But whereas the holy virgin had had to wait for the normal nine months, I needed only seven and a half. Premature birth? Timely abortion? Merely Salome performing a dance of initiation at the Haus der Stille und Besinnung in Kappel am Albis. Johannes Møllgaard served as draftsman.

S

"Endings" is a cut from "Braids of Justification," in G. B. Benko, ed., *Space and Social Theory: Towards a Post-Modern Geography* (Ottawa: University of Ottawa Press, 1990). It is lifted from a longer treatment of the crisis of the sign. In June of 1988 the full version was read as a lecture at the Philosophy Department of the Spanish Research Council in Madrid.

"In Parentheses" is the portrait that was hardest to frame.

Finally, this entire exhibition should be viewed together with the landscapes earlier collected in *Antipasti* (Göteborg: Korpen, 1990). The sketches of that volume picture a dominant ideology participating in its own wake. Some of the same pieces have been translated into Danish and issued as *Krisens tegn/Tegnets krise* (Nimtofte: Forlaget Indtryk, 1989).

Where will it lead? Who knows, except perhaps Rrose Sellavy. But it is in that artist never to say, only to show. The smile is hidden under a moustache, the secret stuck in the eyes of the beholder. Ready maid?

Prefigured

And who prefigured them all—Malevich's black icon, Kandinsky's intimate communication, Wittgenstein's solipsist screams, Duchamp's c'est la vie, my own inventions? Several. One was Walt Whitman in his rendering of the four faces of the Godhead. The Father without remorse. The Son absorbed by affection and charity. The Rebel always despised, because always set against the ruler. Holy Spirit, essence of forms, name of the beyond beyond the beyond.

1

Chanting the square deific, out of the One advancing, out of
the sides,
Out of the old and new, out of the square entirely divine,

Solid, four-sided, (all the sides needed,) from this side Jehovah
        am I,
Old Brahm I, and I Saturnius am;
Not Time affects me—I am Thine, old, modern as any,
Unpersuadable, relentless, executing righteous judgments,
As the Earth, the Father, the brown old Kronos, with laws,
Aged beyond computation, yet ever new, ever with those
        mighty laws rolling,
Relentless I forgive no man—whoever sins dies—I will have
        that man's life;
Therefore let none expect mercy—have the seasons, gravita-
        tion, the appointed days, mercy? no more
        have I,
But as the seasons and gravitation, and as all the appointed
        days that forgive not,
I dispense from this side judgments inexorable without the
        least remorse.

2

Consolater most mild, the promis'd one advancing,
With gentle hand extended, the mightier God am I,
Foretold by prophets and poets in their most rapt prophecies
        and poems,
From this side, lo! the Lord Christ gazes—lo! Hermes—I—lo!
        mine is Hercules' face,
All sorrow, labor, suffering, I, tallying it, absorb in myself,
Many times have I been rejected, taunted, put in prison, and
        crucified, and many times shall be again,
All the world have I given up for dear brothers' and sisters'
        sake, for the soul's sake,
Wending my way through the homes of men, rich or poor, with
        the kiss of affection,

For I am affection, I am the cheer-bringing God, with hope
        and all enclosing charity,
With indulgent words as to children, with fresh and sane
        words, mine only,
Young and strong I pass knowing well I am destin'd myself to
        an early death;
But my charity has no death—my wisdom dies not, neither
        early nor late,
And my sweet love bequeath'd here and elsewhere never dies.

3

Aloof, dissatisfied, plotting revolt,
Comrade of criminals, brother of slaves,
Crafty, despised, a drudge, ignorant,
With sudra face and worn brow, black, but in the depths of
        my heart, proud as any,
Lifted now and always against whoever scorning assumes to
        rule me,
Morose, full of guile, full of reminiscenses, brooding, with
        many wiles,
(Though it was thought I was baffled and dispel'd, and my
        wiles done, but that will never be,)
Defiant, I, Satan still live, still utter words, in new lands duly
        appearing, (and old ones also,)
Permanent here from my side, warlike, equal with any, real
        as any,
Nor time nor change shall ever change me or my words.

4

Santa Spirita, breather, life,
Beyond the light, lighter than light,

Beyond the flames of hell, joyous, leaping easily above hell,

Beyond Paradise, perfumed solely with mine own perfume,

Including all life on earth, touching, including God, including
Saviour and Satan,

Ethereal, pervading all, (for without me what were all? what
were God?)

Essence of forms, life of the real identities, permanent, positive, (namely the unseen,)

Life of the great round world, the sun and stars, and of man,
I, the general soul,

Here the square finishing, the solid, I the most solid,

Breathe my breath also through these songs.

Walt Whitman, *Chanting the Square Deific*

INDEX

Proper Names

Chagall, Marc, 114, 150
Cixous, Hélène, 138–39
Couclelis, Helen, 216
Creon, 80–81, 90
Curry, Leslie, 157

Davidson, Donald, 46
Dedalus, Stephen, 48
de Man, Paul, 210
Derrida, Jacques, 36, 46, 112, 117, 139, 140, 142, 174
Descartes, René, 15, 46, 56, 60, 110, 121, 138, 174, 190
Diana, 25, 198–99
Dionysus, 117–18
Dostoevsky, Fyodor, 139–40
Duchamp, Marcel, 18, 111, 190, 219
Dufy, Bruce, 132
Duncan, James S., 217
Durkheim, Emile, 35

Einstein, Alfred, 21, 141
Elias, Norbert, 138
Eliot, T. S., 174
Engels, Friedrich, 19
Epimenides, 110, 168, 171
Euclid, 25, 140, 193

Farinelli, Franco, 4, 25
Feuerbach, Ludwig, 36
Flaubert, Gustave, 131
Foucault, Michel, 47, 97, 101, 117-21, 138
Frege, Gottlob, 32, 116
Freud, Sigmund, 34, 118, 140

Galilei, Galileo, 69
Gass, William H., 116
Geertz, Clifford, 100
Giddens, Anthony, 138
Girard, René, 23, 167, 176, 180
God, 14, 33–34, 71, 103, 145, 171–72, 175, 176
Gogol, Nikolai, 142
Golledge, Reginald, 217
Gould, Peter, 216
Gregory, Derek, 215

Habermas, Jürgen, 105
Hamlet, 48
Harvey, David, 158–59
HCE, 208

Hegel, G. W. F., 21, 22, 35, 36, 37, 67–77, 98, 119, 151, 174, 175, 190
Heidegger, Martin, 140
Hemingway, Ernest, 50, 161
Hintikka, Jaakko, 43–50, 215
Hirdman, Yvonne, 217
Homer, 102, 178
Horkheimer, Max, 100
Husserl, Edmund, 74, 140

Isaac, 172

Janus, 13–26, 117, 191, 198–99
Jensen, Ole Michael, 4, 217
Jocasta, 80–88
Joyce, James, 22, 23, 48, 206, 215
Joyce, John, 215

Kafka, Franz, 112, 172
Kandinsky, Wassily, v, vii, 5–8, 23, 24, 219
Kant, Immanuel, 22, 24, 156, 174, 192
Kierkegaard, Søren, 37, 77, 119, 132, 172, 174
Kristeva, Julia, 132, 138
Kublai Khan, 161
Kyrklund, Willy, 158

Lacan, Jacques, 23, 24, 49, 121, 138, 167, 174, 179
Laios, 77–90, 105
Larsen, Kurt, 149
Leibniz, Gottfried, 31, 73, 98, 171, 189, 190
Luther, Martin, 35

Machado, Antonio, 123
Malevich, Kasimir, 8, 24, 185–96, 197–99, 219
Mallarmé, Stéphane, 23, 24, 47, 50, 107, 109, 156, 158, 176, 177, 181, 206
Marcuse, Herbert, 100
Martins, Ron, 215
Marx, Karl, 19–21, 36, 37, 62, 73, 76, 78, 104, 116, 117, 119, 133, 155–56, 158–59, 179, 189
Meinong, Alexius, 32
Merleau-Ponty, Maurice, 138–40, 145
Møllgaard, Johannes, 4, 217
Mondrian, Piet, 181, 188
Monet, Claude, 5
Moses, 176–77
Musil, Robert, 112, 115

Nietzsche, Friedrich, 14, 36, 47, 56, 112, 119, 121–22, 138, 140, 146–47, 150, 154, 168

Ockham, 15
Odysseus, 96, 107, 178
Oedipus, 77–90, 105
Olsson, Gunnar, 5–8, 23, 25, 30, 54, 214–16, 217
Oracle, 80–81
Oxford English Dictionary, 15, 95

Papageorgiou, Yorgo, 157
Penelope, 110
Péret, Benjamin, 160
Plato, 46, 133, 141, 174
Polo, Marco, 161
Polybos, 82–85
Polyphemos, 96, 178
Popilius, 26
Pred, Allan, 4

Quine, W. V., 32, 48

Ramirez, José Luis, 4
Reichert, Dagmar, 4
Riemann, Bernhard, 21
Rimbaud, Arthur, 177, 206

Russell, Bertrand, 22, 24, 30–31, 47, 73, 98–99

Salome, 217
Samson, 15
Sartre, Jean-Paul, 46
Saussure, Ferdinand de, 24, 60–61, 65, 116, 117, 137, 138, 152, 159, 169, 177, 179, 192
Sellavy, Rrose, 190, 218
Shakespeare, William, 48
Sophocles, 22, 24, 59–60, 77–90
Sphinx, 77
Stalin, Josef, 69, 175
Stein, Gertrude, 189
Stelarc, 146–50

Teiresias, 78–80, 83
Tobler, Waldo, 157

Valéry, Paul, 145

Whitman, Walt, 219–22
Wittgenstein, Ludwig, 19–20, 43, 97, 98, 115, 129–37, 143, 144, 171, 193–94, 217

Zanetto, Gabriel, 217

Gunnar Olsson is professor of economic geography and planning at the Nordic Institute for Studies in Urban and Regional Planning in Stockholm. Olsson was professor of geography at the University of Michigan, and has been a Fellow of the American Council of Learned Societies. Among his books are *Distance and Human Interaction, Birds in Egg/Eggs in Bird,* and *Antipasti*.